Theodore Roosevelt and Reform Politics

JA Hoffmann Jr

1972

PROBLEMS IN AMERICAN CIVILIZATION

Under the editorial direction of
Edwin C. Rozwenc

Theodore Roosevelt and Reform Politics

Edited and with an Introduction by

Richard H. Collin
Louisiana State University
in New Orleans

D. C. HEATH AND COMPANY
Lexington, Massachusetts   Toronto   London

For Henry Bamford Parkes
and my mother and father.

Published simultaneously in Canada.

Printed in the United States of America.

International Standard Book Number: 0-669-73379-2

Lilbrary of Congress Catalog Card Number: 74-171364

CONTENTS

INTRODUCTION

When Theodore Roosevelt assumed the presidency after the assassination of William McKinley in September 1901, there was little question that the nineteenth century had ended and the twentieth century had begun. Roosevelt was clearly the new century's President. With his presidency, a new era of progressive politics began.

Woodrow Wilson, a leading political scientist and the man destined to defeat Roosevelt in the 1912 election, recognized the importance of Roosevelt's presidency in the 1907 revision of his standard government text when, for the first time, he acknowledged that the President could be a powerful force in American government rather than merely a figurehead. As President, Roosevelt had changed the direction and pace of American life. Did he change it for the better? Was the Roosevelt era an era of reform or did it entrench more securely the control of the government by big business interests? Did Roosevelt, by enlarging the role of the federal government, circumvent the powerful reform impulse at the state and local level? Was Roosevelt a liberal, a conservative, or a radical, or was he at times all three? Was he genuinely interested in effective reform or was his progressivism largely a matter of rhetoric? These are some of the issues underlying the problem of Theodore Roosevelt and American reform politics.

The selections in this volume begin with Theodore Roosevelt's own writings and speeches. These are designed to be read in conjunction with the appropriate historical commentaries in Parts III, IV, and V. The first selection in Part I is an excerpt from Roosevelt's annual message to Congress in 1902, in which he called for regulation and control of trusts, a continuous theme throughout his presidency. Roosevelt recognized that large corporate combinations were an inevitable consequence of modern industrialism and that the national government must exercise greater regulatory power over them.

Roosevelt successfully exploited the public distrust of the railroad monopolies and, in 1906, he managed to convince Congress to pass the Hepburn Bill, America's first effective railroad control bill. Railroad reform is central to the entire problem of Roosevelt's role as an effective reformer, and the next selection taken from his speech to the Union League in Philadelphia reveals some of his thinking about the need for reform.

The comments about muckrakers in the next text are sometimes taken as evidence that Roosevelt was not sympathetic to the aims of the leading reformers of his age. The journalist crusaders at the turn of the century were not called *muckrakers* until Roosevelt compared them to Paul Bunyan's man with the muckrake. They defiantly adopted the name and it has stuck with them in history. The final selection in this group of Rooseveltian statements is an excerpt from Roosevelt's annual message to Congress in 1907, in which he discusses the importance of his conservation reform programs, and his underlying belief in conservation.

The second group of Rooseveltian writings contain Roosevelt's progressive ideals as they had matured in his post-presidential years. Progressivism reached its height in the 1912 election when Roosevelt, after failing to receive the Republican nomination, entered the presidential contest as a third party candidate. The first speech included here is one of Roosevelt's most important. Delivered at Osawatomie, Kansas in August 1910, it signaled Roosevelt's philosophical break with the Taft wing of the Republican party. The speech called for a "New Nationalism" that would make human welfare more important than property. Later in the same speaking tour, Roosevelt made his split with the Republican party irreconcilable by demanding the recall of judicial decisions, a notion that horrified conservatives.

The New Nationalism becomes more sharply delineated with the last selection, Roosevelt's Confession of Faith to the Progressive national convention in 1912. Here Roosevelt accepts the nomination of a third party after walking out of the regular Republican convention which had nominated Taft for the presidency. The confession of faith which ends with the exhortation, We stand at Armageddon and we battle for the Lord! reveals much of the evangelical fervor of the Bull Moose Progressive Party.

Part III is divided into two major categories, contemporary judgments of Roosevelt's presidency and later historical judgments. Each selection deals with an aspect of Theodore Roosevelt's role in American reform politics. They attempt to bring into sharper focus the problematic character of Roosevelt's leadership—particularly the relationship between Roosevelt and the progressive movement. The problem of Roosevelt's relation to progressivism is doubly fascinating because contemporary historians are questioning the nature of progressivism and asking whether it was in fact liberalizing in its purposes and consequences. Even Theodore Roosevelt's contemporaries questioned whether some Progressives were interested more in an orderly world than in a just one. The same question is being asked about American liberalism in our own time; the political career of Theodore Roosevelt is relevant to a persistent problem of reform. The selections that follow reveal the sharp disagreements among historians as well as Roosevelt's contemporaries about his role as a reformer and the significance of the progressive movement.

The first selection in Part III was written by Lincoln Steffens, a leading muckraking journalist. Written in 1900 for *McClure's Magazine*, Steffens' article is an interesting analysis of Roosevelt's effectiveness as governor of New York. Steffens reveals the aura of reform that surrounded Roosevelt from the start of his political career, and examines his methods in dealing with machine politicians and corporate lobbyists.

Herbert Croly was one of the leading intellectuals of the progressive movement. In his *The Promise of American Life*, Croly set forth an agenda of reform that would lead America to a fulfillment of its democratic possibilities in the twentieth century. The Croly selection from *The Promise of American Life* is an analysis of Roosevelt's role as an American reformer that pointed the way to the New Nationalism of Roosevelt's post-presidential campaigns.

An early criticism of Roosevelt's role as a reformer is to be found in the next selection from Robert La Follette's *Autobiography*. La

Follette, the brilliant governor and senator from Wisconsin, was one of the prime movers in the progressive reform movement. La Follette posed one of the questions which is central to this book: Was Roosevelt a positive reformer or was he rather a hindrance to other reformers? By 1912 La Follette and Roosevelt were engaged in a bitter struggle for control of the progressive movement. The next selection is by Gifford Pinchot, Roosevelt's chief forester and advisor on conservation. Writing in 1925, Pinchot draws attention to one of the most overlooked aspects of Roosevelt's effectiveness, his skill as an administrator. The selection was written originally as an introduction to one of the volumes of the National Edition of Roosevelt's *Works* in twenty volumes.

The final selection in the first section of Part III is a relatively unknown piece, John Dewey's obituary for the *Dial* on Roosevelt's death in 1919. Dewey, the reformist-philosopher, wrote an unusually perceptive evaluation of Roosevelt's contribution to American reform. Dewey's perspective is particularly valuable because he was clearly one of the avant-garde intellectual reformers in the progressive era.

The historical judgments in Part III are as varied in their assessment of Roosevelt's role as a presidential reformer as are the contemporary views. The first selection in the second section of Part III by the popular historian, Matthew Josephson recalls the criticism of Roosevelt in the excerpt of Robert La Follette. In *President Makers* (1940), Josephson emphasizes the shallowness of Roosevelt's reforming role. Josephson's account seems to reiterate La Follette's view that, whatever the effect of Roosevelt's rhetoric, Roosevelt's presidency in its early phases was not a substantial contribution to reform.

The publication of the monumental edition of Roosevelt's *Letters* in eight volumes between 1951 and 1954 occasioned a revival of interest in Roosevelt's political career. The volumes were issued two at a time and a great deal was written about Roosevelt in scholarly reviews of the *Letters*. John Morton Blum was an associate editor of the *Letters* and at the end of the project he summarized his defense of Roosevelt's role as a reformer in an influential book, *The Republican Roosevelt* (1954). The selection reprinted here deals entirely with the Hepburn Bill (1906); it makes a case for Roosevelt's practical political techniques and takes issue with La Follette's criticism. Blum is Roosevelt's staunchest defender on domestic matters. He bases his argument on Roosevelt's shrewd political pragmatism and insists that the Hepburn Act was a brilliant and effective piece of legislative reform, engineered by the forceful use of presidential power.

Samuel Hays writes of Roosevelt's relation to the conservation movement in a selection from his *Conservation and the Gospel of Efficiency* (1959). Hays tries to separate Roosevelt's moralistic rhetoric from the underlying rationalistic purposes of the conservation crusade. His thesis shows that efficiency and not social welfare was Roosevelt's and the progressives' main inspiration.

The final selection in Part III by Gabriel Kolko questions many of the implications of John Blum's thesis. Kolko argues that Roosevelt actually prevented reform by encouraging an alliance between business interests and a benign federal government under the guise of federal regulation. The selection taken from Kolko's book, *The Triumph of Conservatism* (1963), develops the theme that the progressive era was more conservative than reformist.

Part IV deals with Roosevelt's later career as a Progressive after he left the presidency. Donald Richberg, a lawyer, was an important figure in Roosevelt's new Progressive Party of 1912–1916. Richberg wrote his memoir and analysis of the Bull Moose convention for *Survey* in 1929, little dreaming that he would be called out of private life once more in 1933 to play an even more important role in the New Deal administration under Franklin D. Roosevelt. The selection from Richberg captures the fervor and emotionalism of the Bull Moose crusade and is sympathetic to Roosevelt's basic aims. It is probably the best single account of the Progressive convention of 1912.

Amos Pinchot, the volatile brother of the better-known Gifford draws a different conclusion from the Bull Moose crusade. He is sharply critical of Roosevelt. Amos's criticisms once angered Roosevelt so much that he angrily wrote to Amos, "When I speak of the lunatic fringe, Amos, I am referring specifically to you." Pinchot's analysis is acute. He attacks Roosevelt for embracing the Morgan-

Perkins formula for trust regulation. Pinchot's history takes the form of an historical memoir; it was written in 1927 and recently reissued in a new edition. Much of what Pinchot wrote foreshadowed the more detailed analysis Gabriel Kolko wrote in 1963.

The remaining selections in Part IV are from modern historians who include the 1912 campaign in their assessment of Roosevelt's relation to the progressive movement as a whole. George M. Mowry's *Theodore Roosevelt and the Progressive Movement* appeared in 1946 and remains the only treatment of Roosevelt's post-presidential years prepared from original sources. In this selection Mowry analyzes in detail the hectic 1912 campaign; he compares Roosevelt's Bull Moose style to his earlier political campaigns, and examines many of Roosevelt's speeches. Mowry discusses the relative importance of Roosevelt's program and Roosevelt's personality and concludes that without Roosevelt as its leader, the New Nationalism would have fared poorly at the polls.

Arthur S. Link, the distinguished biographer of Woodrow Wilson and a leading historian of the Progressive Movement, has always been interested in Theodore Roosevelt. Link sees the progressive movement as a continuing force throughout the twentieth century, a movement taking various forms, including prohibition in the 1920's and Franklin D. Roosevelt's New Deal. The selection included here from Link's *Woodrow Wilson and the Progressive Era* examines the conflicting political programs of Woodrow Wilson's New Freedom and Theodore Roosevelt's New Nationalism. Link is concerned with the nuances of political ideology revealed in the 1912 campaign. He examines carefully the maturation of Roosevelt's and Wilson's views. Link examines one of Roosevelt's principal problems in 1912, how to convince voters that his New Nationalism was a sincere program and not merely a campaign scheme to win votes. As popular as Roosevelt was, the Bull Moose leader was unable to swing sufficient progressive sentiment from Wilson to win the election. A fundamental irony of Roosevelt's defeat in 1912 was that the New Nationalism survived and was subsequently adopted by Wilson in 1915 and 1916. By the election of 1916 both of the great progressive programs debated in the 1912 election had become a permanent part of the tradition of American political reform.

Part V deals with Roosevelt's ideas and ideals. Even though he was well read and wrote books of his own, Theodore Roosevelt was not an original thinker. The selections in this last section attempt to explain Roosevelt's aims and his implementation of them.

Richard Hofstadter's changing views of Theodore Roosevelt mirror the changes in recent Roosevelt historiography. In *The American Political Tradition* (1947) Hofstadter severely attacked Roosevelt as a reformer. In *The Age of Reform* (1954) and in a later book *Anti-Intellectualism in American Life* (1963), Hofstadter changes his viewpoint. In this excerpt from the *Age of Reform* Hofstadter explores the reasons why Theodore Roosevelt had such a strong influence on the people and in what manner Rooseveltian progressivism responded to and expressed the needs of the time. The essential conservatism of Roosevelt's presidency, the overwhelming middle class character of the progressive movement, and Roosevelt's success in restoring the people's faith in government are examined. Hofstadter sees the central problem of Roosevelt's time as a fear of power and of extremists. Roosevelt succeeded in calming the fears of the nation and in preventing radicalism from developing by effecting enough reform concessions of a humane character to avoid open class conflict.

Elting E. Morison's essay on Roosevelt's ideals and their relation to the progressive era is a fitting summary to a study of the problem of Theodore Roosevelt and reform. Morison was editor-in-chief of the Roosevelt *Letters* and wrote the introductions to several volumes of *The Letters*. In this selection from Volume 5, Morison argues that Roosevelt's instinctive judgments were remarkably prescient with regard to the policies that the United States needed to pursue in the twentieth century.

Theodore Roosevelt's role in American reform has been difficult to define, both for his contemporaries and for later historians. While virtually all commentators agree that Roosevelt was central to the great reform movement of the twentieth century, the nature of his influence remains open to interpretation. These selections attempt to show the diversity of Roosevelt's reforms, the relation of his presidency to reform, and the part that Roosevelt played in the development of modern American liberalism. The selections also deal with the very nature of reform in twentieth-century America. Were the liberals actually liberal, or is modern American liberalism more conservative than radical? Was liberalism more a style than a substance? What, indeed, were the long-term results of the Roosevelt era in American politics? No longer are students of American history satisfied with the assumption that recent American reform was simply the triumph of the people over the business interests, and that liberalism represented the forces of good in American life battling those of evil. The problems are more complex, the motives less simple. At the center of the paradox of American liberalism and reform lies the complex role of Theodore Roosevelt, whose Square Deal and New Nationalism symbolized the beginnings of modern American reform. It is this movement of reform which historians are agonizingly reevaluating today.

Conflict of Opinion

Roosevelt's Reform: substance or rhetoric?

He made the problem of economic readjustment the problem of the rebuke of unrighteousness. He endued the cause of the reformer with glamour of virility and vitality. . . .

JOHN DEWEY

Each year Roosevelt becomes less impressive in retrospect. . . . There was a Rooseveltian era . . . there was at the same time a Muckraking era, and this was more solidly based in social conscience. Roosevelt was a promise rather than a fulfillment.

LOUIS FILLER

Roosevelt's Reform: The Hepburn Act:

For an orderly administrative system, for the right of efficient federal controls, for the positive government of an industrial society, he mobilized in a crucial first skirmish the full powers of his office. And he won.

JOHN M. BLUM

He acted upon the maxim that half a loaf is better than no bread . . . I believe that half a loaf is fatal whenever it is accepted at the sacrifice of the basic principle sought to be attained. Half a loaf, as a rule, dulls the appetite, and destroys the keenness of interest in attaining the full loaf. . . . [Roosevelt] after a service of seven and one half years . . . left no great constructive statute as an enduring record of his service. After his term . . . the progressive movement made its greatest progress nationally.

ROBERT M. LA FOLLETTE

Roosevelt as Reformer:

Day in and day out during 1906 and most of 1907 . . . Roosevelt gave eloquent voice to the demand for extension of public authority over great aggregations of wealth . . . his leadership of the reform cause was courageous and effective.

ARTHUR S. LINK

. . . Reform to him was a means of preventing radical social change. And inevitably as if by reflex, he identified himself with conservatism and a benevolent paternalism.

GABRIEL KOLKO

The New Nationalism: Control of Business or Protection of Business?

. . . Now as between governmental regulation by forty-five states and governmental regulation by the central authority of the federal government, there can be but one choice. . . . The choice must be that of a federal regulation.

Editorial, *WALL STREET JOURNAL,* 1904

The Morgan interests [were] entrenched . . . in the Roosevelt cabinet, shaped Roosevelt's economic thinking and the pro-trust policy of the industrial sections of his messages to Congress. It had spread through the mouth of the President himself, Morgan's own pet distinction between good and bad trusts, which is still erroneously attributed to Roosevelt instead of Morgan.

AMOS PINCHOT

Mr. Roosevelt has imparted a higher and more positive significance to reform, because throughout his career he has consistently stood for an idea, from which the idea of reform cannot be separated—namely, the national idea.

HERBERT CROLY

I ROOSEVELT'S PRESIDENTIAL PROGRAMS

Theodore Roosevelt

REGULATION OF CORPORATIONS

*This excerpt from Roosevelt's Second Annual Message to Congress reveals
all of Roosevelt's favorite arguments for greater governmental control over
the economy. Roosevelt was fond of moralistic arguments against unregulated corporate power and prone to diatribes against business interests.
His basic position on the trust problem was far less simple than it appeared.
He admired the efficiency of the large corporations and felt that this efficiency was essential to American prosperity. He feared that their immense
size would ultimately allow corporate interests to usurp a disproportionately
large share of political power, power which properly belonged to the
President and Congress. Roosevelt sought to make the federal government
stronger than the corporate interests while still maintaining the efficiency of
the corporate business system. He began his program to strengthen the
presidency by challenging the Northern Securities Company, a merger of
the J. P. Morgan, E. H. Harriman, and James Hill railroad interests, with an
anti-trust suit in 1902. When the Supreme Court ruled in the government's
favor in 1904 Roosevelt had won the first round. Federal regulation of
corporate combinations was a political issue central to Roosevelt's entire
presidency and culminated in the Hepburn Bill of 1906.*

No country has ever occupied a higher plane of material well-being
than ours at the present moment. This well-being is due to no sudden or accidental causes, but to the play of the economic forces in
this country for over a century; to our laws, our sustained and
continuous policies; above all, to the high individual average of our
citizenship. Great fortunes have been won by those who have taken
the lead in this phenomenal industrial development, and most of
these fortunes have been won not by doing evil, but as an incident
to action which has benefited the community as a whole. Never
before has material well-being been so widely diffused among our
people. Great fortunes have been accumulated, and yet in the aggregate these fortunes are small indeed when compared to the wealth
of the people as a whole. The plain people are better off than they
have ever been before. The insurance companies, which are prac-

From James D. Richardson (ed.), *A Compilation of Messages and Papers of the
Presidents, 1789–1909,* revised edition (Washington: Bureau of National Literature
and Art, 1909), pp 6710–6712.
Editor's Note: Supporting footnotes have been deleted from this and all other
selections.

tically mutual benefit societies—especially helpful to men of moderate means—represent accumulations of capital which are among the largest in this country. There are more deposits in the savings-banks, more owners of farms, more well-paid wage-workers in this country now than ever before in our history. Of course, when the conditions have favored the growth of so much that was good, they have also favored somewhat the growth of what was evil. It is eminently necessary that we should endeavor to cut out this evil, but let us keep a due sense of proportion; let us not in fixing our gaze upon the lesser evil forget the greater good. The evils are real and some of them are menacing, but they are the outgrowth, not of misery or decadence, but of prosperity—of the progress of our gigantic industrial development. This industrial development must not be checked, but side by side with it should go such progressive regulation as will diminish the evils. We should fail in our duty if we did not try to remedy the evils, but we shall succeed only if we proceed patiently, with practical common sense as well as resolution, separating the good from the bad and holding on to the former while endeavoring to get rid of the latter.

In my message to the present Congress at its first session I discussed at length the question of the regulation of those big corporations commonly doing an interstate business, often with some tendency to monopoly, which are popularly known as trusts. The experience of the past year has emphasized, in my opinion, the desirability of the steps I then proposed. A fundamental requisite of social efficiency is a high standard of individual energy and excellence; but this is in nowise inconsistent with power to act in combination for aims which cannot so well be achieved by the individual acting alone. A fundamental base of civilization is the inviolability of property; but this is in nowise consistent with the right of society to regulate the exercise of the artificial powers which it confers upon the owners of property, under the name of corporate franchises, in such a way as to prevent the misuse of these powers. Corporations, and especially combinations of corporations, should be managed under public regulation. Experience has shown that under our system of government the necessary supervision cannot be obtained by State action. It must therefore be achieved by national action. Our aim is not to do away with corporations; on the contrary, these big aggregations are an inevitable development of modern industrialism, and the effort to destroy them would be futile unless accomplished in ways that would work the utmost mischief to the entire body politic. We can do nothing of good in the way of regulating and supervising these corporations until we fix clearly in our minds that we are not attacking the corporations, but endeavoring to do away with any evil in them. We are not hostile to them; we are merely determined that they shall be so handled as to subserve the public good. We draw the line against misconduct, not against wealth. The capitalist who, alone or in conjunction with his fellows, performs some great industrial feat by which he wins money is a well-doer, not a wrong-doer, provided only he works in proper and legitimate lines. We wish to favor such a man when he does well. We wish to supervise and control his actions only to prevent him from doing ill. Publicity can do no harm to the honest corporation; and we need not be overtender about sparing the dishonest corporation.

In curbing and regulating the combinations of capital which are, or may become, injurious to the public we must be careful not to stop the great enterprises which have legitimately reduced the cost of production, not to abandon the place which our country has won in the leadership of the international industrial world, not to strike down wealth with the result of closing factories and mines, of turning the wage-worker idle in the streets and leaving the farmer without a market for what he grows. Insistence upon the impossible means delay in achieving the possible, exactly as, on the other hand, the stubborn defense alike of what is good and what is bad in the existing system, the resolute effort to obstruct any attempt at betterment, betrays blindness to the historic truth that wise evolution is the sure safeguard against revolution.

No more important subject can come before the Congress than this of the regulation of interstate business. This country cannot afford to sit supine on the plea that under our peculiar system of government we are helpless in the presence of the new conditions, and unable to grapple with them or to cut out whatever of evil has arisen in connection with them. The power of the Congress to regulate interstate commerce is an absolute and unqualified grant, and without limitations other than those prescribed by the Constitution.

The Congress has constitutional authority to make all laws necessary and proper for executing this power, and I am satisfied that this power has not been exhausted by any legislation now on the statute-books. It is evident, therefore, that evils restrictive of commercial freedom and entailing restraint upon national commerce fall within the regulative power of the Congress and that a wise and reasonable law would be a necessary and proper exercise of congressional authority to the end that such evils should be eradicated.

I believe that monopolies, unjust discriminations, which prevent or cripple competition, fraudulent overcapitalization and other evils in trust organizations and practices which injuriously affect interstate trade can be prevented under the power of the Congress to "regulate commerce with foreign nations and among the several States" through regulations and requirements operating directly upon such commerce, the instrumentalities thereof, and those engaged therein.

I earnestly recommend this subject to the consideration of the Congress with a view to the passage of a law reasonable in its provisions and effective in its operations, upon which the questions can be finally adjudicated that now raise doubts as to the necessity of constitutional amendment. If it prove impossible to accomplish the purposes above set forth by such a law, then, assuredly, we should not shrink from amending the Constitution so as to secure beyond peradventure the power sought.

The Congress has not heretofore made any appropriation for the better enforcement of the antitrust law as it now stands. Very much has been done by the Department of Justice in securing the enforcement of this law, but much more could be done if the Congress would make a special appropriation for this purpose, to be expended under the direction of the attorney-general.

Theodore Roosevelt
UNION LEAGUE SPEECH, 1905

By 1900 the railroad industry had become the most powerful corporate group in America and one of the chief causes of political unrest. As a leader in the merger movement, the railroads had also become a symbol of the arbitrary economic power exercised by huge corporations. Because the Supreme Court had limited the power of the Interstate Commerce Commission, the railroad industry was unchecked by any regulations. It charged discriminatory rates, arbitrarily reduced or discontinued service, and fixed virtually any rates it desired. When Roosevelt won reelection in 1904 he determined to pursue with renewed vigor his campaign to bring corporate power under federal control. Many businessmen had helped Roosevelt in the 1904 presidential campaign; they hoped he would be a more docile chief executive after his reelection. However, Roosevelt was aware of the widespread public disapproval of the power of the railroads. He felt the failure to curb this power would ultimately bring about more radical solutions, even revolution. In this speech Roosevelt challenged the leaders of an exclusive Philadelphia businessman's club to join with him in a program of reasonable reform. The United States Senate at this time was conservative and represented these larger business interests; it declined to compromise and the struggle over a railroad control bill became the most important issue of Roosevelt's second term. Roosevelt gave up virtually all his other reform programs to concentrate on the fight for railroad control. Eventually a compromise measure, the Hepburn Bill, was passed. While it did not go as far as many progressives had hoped, the Hepburn Bill did establish effective governmental control over railroad rates and practices.

Unquestionably the great development of industrialism means that there must be an increase in the supervision exercised by the Government over business enterprises. This supervision should not take the form of violent and ill-advised interference; and assuredly there is danger lest it take such form if the business leaders of the business community confine themselves to trying to thwart the effort at regulation instead of guiding it aright. Such men as the members of this club should lead in the effort to secure proper supervision and regulation of corporate activity by the Government, not only because it is for the interest of the community as a whole that there should be this supervision and regulation, but because in the long run it

From the *New York Times*, January 31, 1905, pp 1, 3.

7

will be in the interest above all of the very people who often betray alarm and anger when the proposition is first made.

Neither this people nor any other free people will permanently tolerate the use of the vast power conferred by vast wealth, and especially by wealth in its corporate form, without lodging somewhere in the Government the still higher power of seeing that this power, in addition to being used in the interest of the individual or individuals possessing it, is also used for and not against the interests of the people as a whole. Our peculiar form of government, a Government in which the Nation is supreme throughout the Union in certain respects, while each of nearly half a hundred States is supreme in its part of the Union in certain other respects, renders the task of dealing with these conditions especially difficult. No finally satisfactory result can be expected from merely State action. The action must come through the Federal Government. The business of the country is now carried on in a way of which the founders of our Constitution could by no possibility have had any idea. . . .

All great business concerns are engaged in inter-State commerce, and it was beyond question the intention of the founders of our Government that inter-State commerce in all its branches and aspects should be under National and not State control. If the courts decide that this intention was not carried out and made effective in the Constitution as it now stands, then in the end the Constitution, if not construed differently, will have to be amended so that the original undoubted intention may be made effective. But, of course, a Constitutional amendment is only to be used as a last resort, if every effort of legislation and administration shall have been proved inadequate.

Meanwhile the men in public life and the men who direct the great business interests of the country should work not in antagonism, but in harmony toward this given end. In entering a field where the progress must of necessity be so largely experimental it is essential that the effort to make progress should be tentative and cautious. We must grow by evolution, not by revolution. There must be no hurry, but there must also be no halt; and those who are anxious that there should be no sudden and violent changes must remember that precisely these sudden and violent changes will be rendered likely if we refuse to make the needed changes in cautious and moderate manner. . . .

At the present moment the greatest need is for an increase in the power of the National Government to keep the great highways of commerce open alike to all on reasonable and equitable terms. Less than a century ago these highways were still, as they had been since the dawn of history, either waterways natural or artificial, or else ordinary roads for wheel vehicles drawn by animal power. The railroad, which was utterly unknown when our Government was formed and when the great principles of our jurisprudence were laid down, has now become almost everywhere the most important, and, in many large regions, the only form of highway for commerce. The man who controls its use cannot be permitted to control it in his own interest alone.

It is not only just but it is in the interest of the public that this man should receive the amplest payment for the masterful business capacity which enables him to benefit himself while benefiting the public; but in return he must himself recognize his duty to the public. He will not and cannot do this if our laws are so defective that in the sharp competition of the business world the conscientious man is put at a disadvantage by his less scrupulous fellows. It is in the interest of the conscientious and public-spirited railway man that there should be such governmental supervision of the railway traffic of this country as to require from his less scrupulous big shippers as well, that heed to the public welfare which he himself would willingly give, and which is of vital consequence to the small shipper. Every important railroad is engaged in inter-State commerce. Therefore, this control over the railroads must come from the National Government. . . .

We do not intend that this Republic shall ever fail as those republics of olden times failed, in which there finally came to be a government by classes, which resulted either in the poor plundering the rich, or in the rich exploiting, and in one form or another enslaving the poor; for either event means the destruction of free institutions and of individual liberty. Ours is not a Government which recognizes classes. It is based on the recognition of the individual. We are not for the poor man as such, nor for the rich man as such.

We are for every man, rich or poor, provided he acts justly and fairly by his fellows, and if he so acts the Government must do all it can to see that inasmuch as he does no wrong, so he shall suffer no wrong. . . .

Theodore Roosevelt
THE MAN WITH THE MUCK-RAKE SPEECH

Theodore Roosevelt's ambivalence toward reform is demonstrated by this attack on the muckrakers. Delivered at the dedication of a new congressional office building, April 14, 1906, this speech gave Roosevelt the occasion to lash out at the critics of his presidency and of American society by comparing them with Paul Bunyan's character in Pilgrim's Progress. *Roosevelt stated his case against journalistic criticism in the strongest personal terms; he called them liars and put them in the same class as thieves. These same writers who had helped Roosevelt push his reform legislation through Congress adopted the term Roosevelt used contemptuously. Muckraking became a synonym for civic-minded reform journalism.*

In Bunyan's *Pilgrim's Progress* you may recall the description of the Man with the Muck-rake, the man who could look no way but downward, with the muck-rake in his hand; who was offered a celestial crown for his muck-rake, but who would neither look up nor regard the crown he was offered, but continued to rake to himself the filth of the floor.

  In *Pilgrim's Progress* the Man with the Muck-rake is set forth as the example of him whose vision is fixed on carnal instead of on spiritual things. Yet he also typifies the man who in this life consistently refuses to see aught that is lofty, and fixes his eyes with solemn intentness only on that which is vile and debasing. Now, it is very necessary that we should not flinch from seeing what is vile and debasing. There is filth on the floor, and it must be scraped up with the muck-rake; and there are times and places where this

From Theodore Roosevelt, *Presidential Addresses and State Papers,* 8 vols. (New York: The Review of Reviews Company, 1910) V, 712–724.

service is the most needed of all the services that can be performed. But the man who never does anything else, who never thinks or speaks or writes, save of his feats with the muck-rake, speedily becomes, not a help to society, not an incitement to good, but one of the most potent forces for evil.

There are, in the body politic, economic and social, many and grave evils, and there is urgent necessity for the sternest war upon them. There should be relentless exposure of and attack upon every evil man whether politician or business man, every evil practice, whether in politics, in business, or in social life. I hail as a benefactor every writer or speaker, every man who, on the platform, or in book, magazine, or newspaper, with merciless severity makes such attack, provided always that he in his turn remembers that the attack is of use only if it is absolutely truthful. The liar is no whit better than the thief, and if his mendacity takes the form of slander, he may be worse than most thieves. It puts a premium upon knavery untruthfully to attack an honest man, or even with hysterical exaggeration to assail a bad man with untruth. An epidemic of indiscriminate assault upon character does not good, but very great harm. The soul of every scoundrel is gladdened whenever an honest man is assailed, or even when a scoundrel is untruthfully assailed.

Now, it is easy to twist out of shape what I have just said, easy to affect to misunderstand it, and, if it is slurred over in repetition, not difficult really to misunderstand it. Some persons are sincerely incapable of understanding that to denounce mud-slinging does not mean the indorsement of whitewashing; and both the interested individuals who need whitewashing, and those others who practise mud-slinging, like to encourage such confusion of ideas. One of the chief counts against those who make indiscriminate assault upon men in business or men in public life, is that they invite a reaction which is sure to tell powerfully in favor of the unscrupulous scoundrel who really ought to be attacked, who ought to be exposed, who ought, if possible, to be put in the penitentiary. If Aristides is praised overmuch as just, people get tired of hearing it; and overcensure of the unjust finally and from similar reasons results in their favor.

Any excess is almost sure to invite a reaction; and, unfortunately, the reaction, instead of taking the form of punishment of those guilty of the excess, is very apt to take the form either of punishment of the unoffending or of giving immunity, and even strength, to offenders. The effort to make financial or political profit out of the destruction of character can only result in public calamity. Gross and reckless assaults on character, whether on the stump or in newspaper, magazine, or book, create a morbid and vicious public sentiment, and at the same time act as a profound deterrent to able men of normal sensitiveness and tend to prevent them from entering the public service at any price. As an instance in point, I may mention that one serious difficulty encountered in getting the right type of men to dig the Panama Canal is the certainty that they will be exposed, both without, and, I am sorry to say, sometimes within, Congress, to utterly reckless assaults on their character and capacity.

At the risk of repetition let me say again that my plea is, not for immunity to but for the most unsparing exposure of the politician who betrays his trust, of the big business man who makes or spends his fortune in illegitimate or corrupt ways. There should be a resolute effort to hunt every such man out of the position he has disgraced. Expose the crime, and hunt down the criminal; but remember that even in the case of crime, if it is attacked in sensational, lurid, and untruthful fashion, the attack may do more damage to the public mind than the crime itself. It is because I feel that there should be no rest in the endless war against the forces of evil that I ask that the war be conducted with sanity as well as with resolution. The men with the muck-rakes are often indispensable to the well-being of society; but only if they know when to stop raking the muck, and to look upward to the celestial crown above them, to the crown of worthy endeavor. There are beautiful things above and roundabout them; and if they gradually grow to feel that the whole world is nothing but muck, their power of usefulness is gone. If the whole picture is painted black there remains no hue whereby to single out the rascals for distinction from their fellows. Such painting finally induces a kind of moral color-blindness; and people affected by it come to the conclusion that no man is really black, and no man really white, but they are all gray. In other words, they neither believe in the truth of the attack, nor in the honesty of the man who is attacked; they grow as suspicious of the accusation as of the offense; it becomes well-nigh hopeless to stir them either to wrath against wrong-doing or to enthusiasm for what is right; and such a mental attitude in the public gives hope to every knave, and is the despair of honest men.

To assail the great and admitted evils of our political and industrial life with such crude and sweeping generalizations as to include decent men in the general condemnation means the searing of the public conscience. There results a general attitude either of cynical belief in and indifference to public corruption or else of a distrustful inability to discriminate between the good and the bad. Either attitude is fraught with untold damage to the country as a whole. The fool who has not sense to discriminate between what is good and what is bad is well-nigh as dangerous as the man who does discriminate and yet chooses the bad. There is nothing more distressing to every good patriot, to every good American, than the hard, scoffing spirit which treats the allegation of dishonesty in a public man as a cause for laughter. Such laughter is worse than the crackling of thorns under a pot, for it denotes not merely the vacant mind, but the heart in which high emotions have been choked before they could grow to fruition.

There is any amount of good in the world, and there never was a time when loftier and more disinterested work for the betterment of mankind was being done than now. The forces that tend for evil are great and terrible, but the forces of truth and love and courage and honesty and generosity and sympathy are also stronger than ever before. It is a foolish and timid, no less than a wicked, thing to blink the fact that the forces of evil are strong, but it is even worse to fail to take into account the strength of the forces that tell for good. Hysterical sensationalism is the very poorest weapon wherewith to fight for lasting righteousness. The men who with stern sobriety and truth assail the many evils of our time, whether in the public press, or in magazines, or in books, are the leaders and allies of all engaged in the work for social and political betterment. But if they give good reason for distrust of what they say, if they chill the ardor of those who demand truth as a primary virtue, they thereby betray the good cause, and play into the hands of the very men against whom they are nominally at war. . . .

It is a prime necessity that if the present unrest is to result in permanent good the emotion shall be translated into action, and that the action shall be marked by honesty, sanity, and self-restraint. There is mighty little good in a mere spasm of reform. The reform that counts is that which comes through steady, continuous growth; violent emotionalism leads to exhaustion.

It is important to this people to grapple with the problems connected with the amassing of enormous fortunes, and the use of those fortunes, both corporate and individual, in business. We should discriminate in the sharpest way between fortunes well-won and fortunes ill-won; between those gained as an incident to performing great services to the community as a whole, and those gained in evil fashion by keeping just within the limits of mere law-honesty. Of course no amount of charity in spending such fortunes in any way compensates for misconduct in making them. As a matter of personal conviction, and without pretending to discuss the details or formulate the system, I feel that we shall ultimately have to consider the adoption of some such scheme as that of a progressive tax on all fortunes, beyond a certain amount either given in life or devised or bequeathed upon death to any individual—a tax so framed as to put it out of the power of the owner of one of these enormous fortunes to hand on more than a certain amount to any one individual; the tax, of course, to be imposed by the National and not the State Government. Such taxation should, of course, be aimed merely at the inheritance or transmission in their entirety of those fortunes swollen beyond all healthy limits. . . .

The only public servant who can be trusted honestly to protect the rights of the public against the misdeed of a corporation is that public man who will just as surely protect the corporation itself from wrongful aggression. If a public man is willing to yield to popular clamor and do wrong to the men of wealth or to rich corporations, it may be set down as certain that if the opportunity comes he will secretly and furtively do wrong to the public in the interest of a corporation.

But, in addition to honesty, we need sanity. No honesty will make a public man useful if that man is timid or foolish, if he is a hot-headed zealot or an impracticable visionary. As we strive for reform we find that it is not at all merely the case of a long up-hill pull. On the contrary, there is almost as much of breeching work as of collar work; to depend only on traces means that there will soon be a runaway and an upset. The men of wealth who today are trying to prevent the regulation and control of their business in the interest of the public by the proper government authorities will not succeed, in my judgment, in checking the progress of the movement. But if they did succeed they would find that they had sown the wind and would surely reap the whirlwind, for they would ultimately provoke the violent excesses which accompany a reform coming by convulsion instead of by steady and natural growth.

On the other hand, the wild preachers of unrest and discontent, the wild agitators against the entire existing order, the men who act crookedly, whether because of sinister design or from mere puzzle-headedness, the men who preach destruction without proposing any substitute for what they intend to destroy, or who propose a substitute which would be far worse than the existing evils—all these men are the most dangerous opponents of real reform. If they get their way they will lead the people into a deeper pit than any into which they could fall under the present system. If they fail to get their way they will still do incalculable harm by provoking the kind of reaction which, in its revolt against the senseless evil of their teaching, would enthrone more securely than ever the very evils which their misguided followers believe they are attacking.

More important than aught else is the development of the broadest sympathy of man for man. The welfare of the wage-worker, the welfare of the tiller of the soil, upon these depend the welfare of the entire country; their good is not to be sought in pulling down others; but their good must be the prime object of all our statesmanship.

Materially we must strive to secure a broader economic opportunity for all men, so that each shall have a better chance to show the stuff of which he is made. Spiritually and ethically we must strive to bring about clean living and right thinking. We appreciate that the things of the body are important; but we appreciate also that the things of the soul are immeasurably more important. The foundation-stone of national life is, and ever must be, the high individual character of the average citizen.

Theodore Roosevelt
CONSERVATION

Throughout his presidency Roosevelt consistently championed conservation reform. He helped preserve the national forests from exploitation and destruction, introduced irrigation and reclamation in the arid West, established wild life sanctuaries, and constantly warned against the dangerous misuse of America's natural resources. By establishing the Inland Waterways Commission and publicizing its findings, Roosevelt began a crusade to preserve the nation's rivers that is still being carried on today. And when he convened the Governors' Conference on Conservation in 1908, Roosevelt inspired in many local leaders the zeal for conservation he himself felt. In this selection from Roosevelt's next to last annual message to Congress, Roosevelt movingly set forth his principles concerning America's natural resources. Like most of Roosevelt's conservation messages it is highly moralistic in tone. However, it also reveals that the core of Roosevelt's program was, above all, practical. He sought a more democratic as well as a more efficient use of America's resources. He was not concerned simply with saving the forests; rather he sought a fair and sensible use of them to benefit not simply a single group or industry but the nation as a whole.

Optimism is a good characteristic, but if carried to an excess it becomes foolishness. We are prone to speak of the resources of this country as inexhaustible; this is not so. The mineral wealth of the country, the coal, iron, oil, gas, and the like, does not reproduce itself, and therefore is certain to be exhausted ultimately; and wastefulness in dealing with it today means that our descendants will feel the exhaustion a generation or two before they otherwise would. But there are certain other forms of waste which could be entirely stopped—the waste of soil by washing, for instance, which is among the most dangerous of all wastes now in progress in the United States, is easily preventable, so that this present enormous loss of fertility is entirely unnecessary. The preservation or replacement of the forests is one of the most important means of preventing this loss. We have made a beginning in forest preservation, but it is only a beginning. At present lumbering is the fourth greatest industry in the United States; and yet, so rapid has been the rate of

From James D. Richardson (ed.), *A Compilation of Messages and Papers of the Presidents, 1789–1909,* revised edition (Washington: Bureau of National Literature and Art, 1909), pp. 7097–7100.

exhaustion of timber in the United States in the past, and so rapidly is the remainder being exhausted, that the country is unquestionably on the verge of a timber famine which will be felt in every household in the land. There has already been a rise in the price of lumber, but there is certain to be a more rapid and heavier rise in the future. The present annual consumption of lumber is certainly three times as great as the annual growth; and if the consumption and growth continue unchanged, practically all our lumber will be exhausted in another generation, while long before the limit to complete exhaustion is reached the growing scarcity will make itself felt in many blighting ways upon our national welfare. About twenty per cent of our forested territory is now reserved in national forests; but these do not include the most valuable timberlands, and in any event the proportion is too small to expect that the reserves can accomplish more than a mitigation of the trouble which is ahead for the nation. Far more drastic action is needed. Forests can be lumbered so as to give to the public the full use of their mercantile timber without the slightest detriment to the forest, any more than it is a detriment to a farm to furnish a harvest; so that there is no parallel between forests and mines, which can only be completely used by exhaustion. But forests, if used as all our forests have been used in the past and as most of them are still used, will be either wholly destroyed, or so damaged that many decades have to pass before effective use can be made of them again. All these facts are so obvious that it is extraordinary that it should be necessary to repeat them. Every businessman in the land, every writer in the newspapers, every man or woman of an ordinary school education, ought to be able to see that immense quantities of timber are used in the country, that the forests which supply this timber are rapidly being exhausted, and that, if no change takes place, exhaustion will come comparatively soon, and that the effects of it will be felt severely in the everyday life of our people. Surely, when these facts are so obvious, there should be no delay in taking preventive measures. Yet we seem as a nation to be willing to proceed in this matter with happy-go-lucky indifference even to the immediate future. It is this attitude which permits the self-interest of a very few persons to weigh for more than the ultimate interest of all our people. There are persons who find it to their immense pecuniary benefit to destroy the forests by lumbering. They are to be blamed for thus sacrificing the future of the nation as a whole to their own self-interest of the moment; but heavier blame attaches to the people at large for permitting such action, whether in the White Mountains, in the southern Alleghanies, or in the Rockies and Sierras. A big lumbering company, impatient for immediate returns and not caring to look far enough ahead, will often deliberately destroy all the good timber in a region, hoping afterward to move on to some new country. The shiftless man of small means, who does not care to become an actual home-maker but would like immediate profit, will find it to his advantage to take up timberland simply to turn it over to such a big company, and leave it valueless for future settlers. A big mine-owner, anxious only to develop his mine at the moment, will care only to cut all the timber that he wishes without regard to the future—probably not looking ahead to the condition of the country when the forests are exhausted, any more than he does to the condition when the mine is worked out. I do not blame these men nearly as much as I blame the supine public opinion, the indifferent public opinion, which permits their action to go unchecked. Of course to check the waste of timber means that there must be on the part of the public the acceptance of a temporary restriction in the lavish use of the timber, in order to prevent the total loss of this use in the future. There are plenty of men in public and private life who actually advocate the continuance of the present system of unchecked and wasteful extravagance, using as an argument the fact that to check it will of course mean interference with the ease and comfort of certain people who now get lumber at less cost than they ought to pay, at the expense of the future generations. Some of these persons actually demand that the present forest reserves be thrown open to destruction, because, forsooth, they think that thereby the price of lumber could be put down again for two or three or more years. Their attitude is precisely like that of an agitator protesting against the outlay of money by farmers on manure and in taking care of their farms generally. Undoubtedly, if the average farmer were content absolutely to ruin his farm, he could for two or three years avoid spending any money on it, and yet make a good deal of money out of it. But only a savage would, in his private affairs, show such reckless disregard of the future; yet it is precisely this reckless disregard of the future which the opponents of the forestry system are now endeavoring to get the people of the United States to show. The only trouble with the movement for the preservation of our forests is that it has not gone nearly far enough, and was not begun soon enough. It is a most fortunate thing, however, that we began it when we did. We should acquire in the Appalachian and White Mountain regions all the forest-lands that it is possible to acquire for the use of the nation. These lands, because they form a national asset, are as emphatically national as the rivers which they feed, and which flow through so many States before they reach the ocean.

There should be no tariff on any forest product grown in this country; and, in especial, there should be no tariff on woodpulp; due notice of the change being of course given to those engaged in the business so as to enable them to adjust themselves to the new conditions. The repeal of the duty on woodpulp should if possible be accompanied by an agreement with Canada that there shall be no export duty on Canadian pulpwood.

II ROOSEVELT'S NEW NATIONALISM

Theodore Roosevelt

THE NEW NATIONALISM, 1910

When Roosevelt was elected President in 1904 he pledged not to run for reelection in 1908, a promise many critics doubted he would keep. Roosevelt did keep his word and after handpicking his successor, William Howard Taft, retired from active American politics for two years. During this time he hunted in Africa and toured Europe. Roosevelt appeared no longer interested in the practical world of politics; he yearned for the role of elder statesman and preacher. But Taft was unable to hold the tenuous Republican coalition together. When Roosevelt returned from Europe in 1910 he found the Republican Party a shambles; the conservatives led by Taft were at war with the progressives who looked to a reluctant Roosevelt for leadership. Roosevelt hoped to patch up the split and bring Taft back to a more progressive political program. Roosevelt at this time was more concerned with making known his new views than in actively seeking political office. This speech at Osawatomie, Kansas on August 31, 1910 marked the end of any possible reconciliation between the Roosevelt and Taft wings of the Republican Party. Roosevelt enunciated for the first time his program, The New Nationalism, which called for a strong central government, the preservation of the corporate system with federal regulation, and the primacy of human rights over property rights. Roosevelt's speech infuriated the conservatives; his program led to his ultimate break with the Republican Party and to the election of 1912 in which Roosevelt's New Nationalism was challenged by Woodrow Wilson's New Freedom. Wilson won the election; Roosevelt finished second. But the New Nationalism outlived the campaign and ultimately was adopted by Wilson in 1915. Many historians consider that the New Nationalism set the pattern for American liberal political programs after Roosevelt's time.

We come here today to commemorate one of the epoch-making events of the long struggle for the rights of man—the long struggle for the uplift of humanity. Our country—this great Republic—means nothing unless it means the triumph of a real democracy, the triumph of popular government, and, in the long run, of an economic system under which each man shall be guaranteed the opportunity to show the best that there is in him. That is why the history of America is now the central feature of the history of the world; for the world has

From Theodore Roosevelt, *The New Nationalism* (New York: The Outlook Co., 1910), pp. 3–33.

set its face hopefully toward our democracy; and, O my fellow citizens, each one of you carries on your shoulders not only the burden of doing well for the sake of your own country, but the burden of doing well and of seeing that this nation does well for the sake of mankind. . . .

I do not speak of this struggle of the past merely from the historic standpoint. Our interest is primarily in the application today of the lessons taught by the contest of half a century ago. It is of little use for us to pay lip-loyalty to the mighty men of the past unless we sincerely endeavor to apply to the problems of the present precisely the qualities which in other crises enabled the men of that day to meet those crises. It is half melancholy and half amusing to see the way in which well-meaning people gather to do honor to the men who, in company with John Brown, and under the lead of Abraham Lincoln, faced and solved the great problems of the nineteenth century, while, at the same time, these same good people nervously shrink from, or frantically denounce, those who are trying to meet the problems of the twentieth century in the spirit which was accountable for the successful solution of the problems of Lincoln's time.

Of that generation of men to whom we owe so much, the man to whom we owe most is, of course, Lincoln. Part of our debt to him is because he forecast our present struggle and saw the way out. He said:

"I hold that while man exists it is his duty to improve not only his own condition, but to assist in ameliorating mankind."

And again:

"Labor is prior to, and independent of, capital. Capital is only the fruit of labor, and could never have existed if labor had not first existed. Labor is the superior of capital, and deserves much the higher consideration."

If that remark was original with me, I should be even more strongly denounced as a Communist agitator than I shall be anyhow. It is Lincoln's. I am only quoting it; and that is one side; that is the side the capitalist should hear. Now, let the working man hear his side.

"Capital has its rights, which are as worthy of protection as any other rights. . . . Nor should this lead to a war upon the owners of property. Property is the fruit of labor; . . . property is desirable; is a positive good in the world."

And then comes a thoroughly Lincolnlike sentence:

"Let not him who is houseless pull down the house of another, but let him work diligently and build one for himself, thus by example assuring that his own shall be safe from violence when built."

It seems to me that, in these words, Lincoln took substantially the attitude that we ought to take; he showed the proper sense of proportion in his relative estimates of capital and labor, of human rights and property rights. Above all, in this speech, as in many others, he taught a lesson in wise kindliness and charity; an indispensable lesson to us of today. But this wise kindliness and charity never weakened his arm or numbed his heart. We cannot afford weakly to blind ourselves to the actual conflict which faces us today. The issue is joined, and we must fight or fail. . . .

Practical equality of opportunity for all citizens, when we achieve it, will have two great results. First, every man will have a fair chance to make of himself all that in him lies; to reach the highest point to which his capacities, unassisted by special privilege of his own and unhampered by the special privilege of others, can carry him, and to get for himself and his family substantially what he has earned. Second, equality of opportunity means that the commonwealth will get from every citizen the highest service of which he is capable. No man who carries the burden of the special privileges of another can give to the commonwealth that service to which it is fairly entitled.

I stand for the square deal. But when I say that I am for the square deal, I mean not merely that I stand for fair play under the present rules of the game, but that I stand for having those rules changed so as to work for a more substantial equality of opportunity and of reward for equally good service. One word of warning, which, I think, is hardly necessary in Kansas. When I say I want a square deal for the poor man, I do not mean that I want a square deal for the man who remains poor because he has not got the energy to work for himself. If a man who has had a chance will not make good, then he has got to quit. And you men of the Grand Army, you want justice for the brave man who fought, and punishment for the coward who shirked his work. Is not that so?

Now, this means that our government, National and State, must be freed from the sinister influence or control of special interests. Exactly as the special interests of cotton and slavery threatened our political integrity before the Civil War, so now the great special business interests too often control and corrupt the men and methods of government for their own profit. We must drive the special interests out of politics. That is one of our tasks today. Every special interest is entitled to justice—full, fair, and complete—and, now, mind you, if there were any attempt by mob-violence to plunder and work harm to the special interest, whatever it may be, that I most dislike, and the wealthy man, whomsoever he may be, for whom I have the greatest contempt, I would fight for him, and you would if you were worth your salt. He should have justice. For every special interest is entitled to justice, but not one is entitled to a vote in Congress, to a voice on the bench, or to representation in any public office. The Constitution guarantees protection to property, and we must make that promise good. But it does not give the right of suffrage to any corporation.

The true friend of property, the true conservative, is he who insists that property shall be the servant and not the master of the commonwealth; who insists that the creature of man's making shall be the servant and not the master of the man who made it. The citizens of the United States must effectively control the mighty commercial forces which they have themselves called into being.

There can be no effective control of corporations while their political activity remains. To put an end to it will be neither a short nor an easy task, but it can be done.

We must have complete and effective publicity of corporate affairs, so that the people may know beyond peradventure whether the corporations obey the law and whether their management entitles them to the confidence of the public. It is necessary that laws should be passed to prohibit the use of corporate funds directly or indirectly for political purposes; it is still more necessary that such laws should be thoroughly enforced. Corporate expenditures for political purposes, and especially such expenditures by public-service corporations, have supplied one of the principal sources of corruption in our political affairs. . . .

Nothing is more true than that excess of every kind is followed by reaction; a fact which should be pondered by reformer and reactionary alike. We are face to face with new conceptions of the relations of property to human welfare, chiefly because certain advocates of the rights of property as against the rights of men have been pushing their claims too far. The man who wrongly holds that every human right is secondary to his profit must now give way to the advocate of human welfare, who rightly maintains that every man holds his property subject to the general right of the community to regulate its use to whatever degree the public welfare may require it.

But I think we may go still further. The right to regulate the use of wealth in the public interest is universally admitted. Let us admit also the right to regulate the terms and conditions of labor, which is the chief element of wealth, directly in the interest of the common good. The fundamental thing to do for every man is to give him a chance to reach a place in which he will make the greatest possible contribution to the public welfare. Understand what I say there. Give him a chance, not push him up if he will not be pushed. Help any man who stumbles; if he lies down, it is a poor job to try to carry him; but if he is a worthy man, try your best to see that he gets a chance to show the worth that is in him. No man can be a good citizen unless he has a wage more than sufficient to cover the bare cost of living, and hours of labor short enough so that after his day's work is done he will have time and energy to bear his share in the management of the community, to help in carrying the general load. We keep countless men from being good citizens by the conditions of life with which we surround them. We need comprehensive workmen's compensation acts, both State and National laws to regulate child labor and work for women, and, especially, we need in our common schools not merely education in book-learning, but also practical training for daily life and work. We need to enforce better sanitary conditions for our workers and to extend the use of safety appliances for our workers in industry and commerce, both within and between the States. Also, friends, in the interest of the working man himself we need to set our faces like flint against mob-violence just as against corporate greed; against violence and injustice and lawlessness by wage-workers just as much as against lawless cunning and greed and selfish arrogance of employers. If I could ask but one thing of my fellow countrymen, my request would be that, whenever they go in for reform, they remember the two sides, and that they always exact justice from one side as much as from the other. I have small use for the public servant who can always see and denounce the corruption of the capitalist, but who cannot persuade himself, especially before election, to say a word about lawless mob-violence. And I have equally small use for the man, be he a judge on the bench, or editor of a great paper, or wealthy and influential private citizen, who can see clearly enough and denounce the lawlessness of mob-violence, but whose eyes are closed so that he is blind when the question is one of corruption in business on a gigantic scale. Also remember what I said about excess in reformer and reactionary alike. If the reactionary man, who thinks of nothing but the rights of property, could have his way, he would bring about a revolution; and one of my chief fears in connection with progress comes because I do not want to see our people, for lack of proper leadership, compelled to follow men whose intentions are excellent, but whose eyes are a little too wild to make it really safe to trust them. Here in Kansas there is one paper which habitually denounces me as the tool of Wall Street, and at the same time frantically repudiates the statement that I am a Socialist on the ground that that is an unwarranted slander of the Socialists.

National efficiency has many factors. It is a necessary result of the principle of conservation widely applied. In the end it will determine our failure or success as a nation. National efficiency has to do, not only with natural resources and with men, but it is equally concerned with institutions. The State must be made efficient for the work which concerns only the people of the State; and the nation for that which concerns all the people. There must remain no neutral ground to serve as a refuge for lawbreakers, and especially for lawbreakers of great wealth, who can hire the vulpine legal cunning which will teach them how to avoid both jurisdictions. It is a misfortune when the National Legislature fails to do its duty in providing a national remedy, so that the only national activity is the purely negative activity of the judiciary in forbidding the State to exercise power in the premises.

I do not ask for overcentralization; but I do ask that we work in a spirit of broad and far-reaching nationalism when we work for what concerns our people as a whole. We are all Americans. Our common interests are as broad as the continent. I speak to you here in Kansas exactly as I would speak in New York or Georgia, for the most vital problems are those which affect us all alike. The National Government belongs to the whole American people, and where the whole American people are interested, that interest can be guarded effectively only by the National Government. The betterment which we seek must be accomplished, I believe, mainly through the National Government.

The American people are right in demanding that New Nationalism, without which we cannot hope to deal with new problems. The New Nationalism puts the national need before sectional or personal advantage. It is impatient of the utter confusion that results from local legislatures attempting to treat national issues as local issues. It is still more impatient of the impotence which springs from overdivision of governmental powers, the impotence which makes it possible for local selfishness or for legal cunning, hired by wealthy special interests, to bring national activities to a deadlock. This New Nationalism regards the executive power as the steward of the public welfare. It demands of the judiciary that it shall be interested primarily In human welfare rather than in property, just as it demands that the representative body shall represent all the people rather than any one class or section of the people.

I believe in shaping the ends of government to protect property as well as human welfare. Normally, and in the long run, the ends are the same; but whenever the alternative must be faced, I am for men and not for property, as you were in the Civil War. I am far from underestimating the importance of dividends; but I rank dividends below human character. Again, I do not have any sympathy with the reformer who says he does not care for dividends. Of course, economic welfare is necessary, for a man must pull his own weight and be able to support his family. I know well that the reformers must not bring upon the people economic ruin, or the reforms themselves will go down in the ruin. But we must be ready to face temporary disaster, whether or not brought on by those who will war against us to the knife. Those who oppose all reform will do well to remember that ruin in its worst form is inevitable if our national life brings us nothing better than swollen fortunes for the few and the triumph in both politics and business of a sordid and selfish materialism.

If our political institutions were perfect, they would absolutely prevent the political domination of money in any part of our affairs. We need to make our political representatives more quickly and sensitively responsive to the people whose servants they are. More direct action by the people in their own affairs under proper safeguards is vitally necessary. The direct primary is a step in this direction, if it is associated with a corrupt-practices act effective to prevent the advantage of the man willing recklessly and unscrupulously to spend money over his more honest competitor. It is particularly important that all moneys received or expended for campaign purposes should be publicly accounted for, not only after election, but before election as well. Political action must be made simpler, easier, and freer from confusion for every citizen. I believe that the prompt removal of unfaithful or incompetent public servants should be made easy and sure in whatever way experience shall show to be most expedient in any given class of cases.

One of the fundamental necessities in a representative government such as ours is to make certain that the men to whom the people delegate their power shall serve the people by whom they are elected, and not the special interests. I believe that every national officer, elected or appointed, should be forbidden to perform any service or receive any compensation, directly or indirectly, from interstate corporations; and a similar provision could not fail to be useful within the States.

The object of government is the welfare of the people. The material progress and prosperity of a nation are desirable chiefly so far as they lead to the moral and material welfare of all good citizens. Just in proportion as the average man and woman are honest, capable of sound judgment and high ideals, active in public affairs—but, first of all, sound in their home life, and the father and mother of healthy children whom they bring up well—just so far, and no farther, we may count our civilization a success. We must have—I believe we have already—a genuine and permanent moral awakening, without which no wisdom of legislation or administration really means anything; and, on the other hand, we must try to secure the social and economic legislation without which any improvement due to purely moral agitation is necessarily evanescent. Let me again illustrate by a reference to the Grand Army. You could not have won simply as a disorderly and disorganized mob. You needed generals; you needed careful administration of the most advanced type; and a good commissary—the cracker line. You well remember that success was necessary in many different lines in order to bring about general success. You had to have the administration at Washington good, just as you had to have the administration in the field; and you had to have the work of the generals good. You could not have triumphed without that administration and leadership; but it would all have been worthless if the average soldier had not had the right stuff in him. He had to have the right stuff in him, or you could not get it out of him. In the last analysis, therefore, vitally necessary though it was to have the right kind of organization and the right kind of generalship, it was even more vitally necessary that the average soldier should have the fighting edge, the right character. So it is in our civil life. No matter how honest and decent we are in our private lives, if we do not have the right kind of law and the right kind of administration of the law, we cannot go forward as a nation. That is imperative; but it must be an addition to, and not a substitution for, the qualities that make us good citizens. In the last analysis, the most important elements in any man's career must be the sum of those qualities which, in the aggregate, we speak of as character. If he has not got it, then no law that the wit of man can devise, no administration of the law by the boldest and strongest executive, will avail to help him. We must have the right kind of character—character that makes a man, first of all, a good man in the home, a good father, a good husband—that makes a man a good neighbor. You must have that, and, then, in addition, you must have the kind of law and the kind of administration of the law which will give to those qualities in the private citizen the best possible chance for development. The prime problem of our nation is to get the right type of good citizenship, and, to get it, we must have progress, and our public men must be genuinely progressive.

Theodore Roosevelt

A CONFESSION OF FAITH, 1912

In June 1912, Roosevelt and his followers dramatically withdrew from a Republican convention that had repudiated its former leader and nominated William Howard Taft. Roosevelt may have been politically motivated in breaking away from the party in June, since the Democrats had not yet chosen a candidate. If the Democratic choice had been a conservative such as Champ Clark, Roosevelt would have had an excellent chance to capture the predominantly progressive sentiment of the nation while Taft and Clark split the conservative vote. However, when Woodrow Wilson won the Democratic nomination Roosevelt had almost no chance to win. Roosevelt and the Progressives went ahead with their third party meeting in Chicago that August. The ensuing political campaign seemed more like a religious revival than a practical political campaign. In this address to the Progressive convention Roosevelt set the tone of the campaign. He proposed the political program of the New Nationalism and exhorted his followers to stand at Armageddon and battle for the Lord. The campaign itself was one of the rare American political confrontations in which fundamental issues and political principles were debated—Wilson's New Freedom vs. Roosevelt's New Nationalism. The fervid evangelism of the Progressives went hand in hand with the philosophical debate. At this American presidential nominating convention a Confession of Faith seemed to fit the occasion.

To you, men and women who have come here to this great city of this great State formally to launch a new party, a party of the people of the whole Union, the National Progressive party, I extend my hearty greeting. You are taking a bold and a greatly needed step for the service of our beloved country. The old parties are husks, with no real soul within either, divided on artificial lines, boss-ridden and privilege-controlled, each a jumble of incongruous elements, and neither daring to speak out wisely and fearlessly what should be said on the vital issues of the day. This new movement is a movement of truth, sincerity, and wisdom, a movement which proposes to put at the service of all our people the collective power of the people, through their governmental agencies, alike in the nation and in the several States. We propose boldly to face the real and great questions of the day, and not skilfully to evade them as do the old parties. We propose to raise aloft a standard to which

From Theodore Roosevelt, *Progressive Principles* (New York: 1913), pp. 115–173.

all honest men can repair, and under which all can fight, no matter what their past political differences, if they are content to face the future and no longer to dwell among the dead issues of the past. We propose to put forth a platform which shall not be a platform of the ordinary and insincere kind, but shall be a contract with the people; and, if the people accept this contract by putting us in power, we shall hold ourselves under honorable obligation to fulfil every promise it contains as loyally as if it were actually enforceable under the penalties of the law.

The prime need today is to face the fact that we are now in the midst of a great economic evolution. There is urgent necessity of applying both common sense and the highest ethical standard to this movement for better economic conditions among the mass of our people if we are to make it one of healthy evolution and not one of revolution. It is, from the standpoint of our country, wicked as well as foolish longer to refuse to face the real issues of the day. Only by so facing them can we go forward; and to do this we must break up the old party organizations and obliterate the old cleavage lines on the dead issues inherited from fifty years ago.

Our fight is a fundamental fight against both of the old corrupt party machines, for both are under the dominion of the plunder league of the professional politicians who are controlled and sustained by the great beneficiaries of privilege and reaction. How close is the alliance between the two machines is shown by the attitude of that portion of those northeastern newspapers, including the majority of the great dailies in all the northeastern cities—Boston, Buffalo, Springfield, Hartford, Philadelphia, and, above all, New York—which are controlled by or representative of the interests which, in popular phrase, are conveniently grouped together as the Wall Street interests. The large majority of these papers supported Judge Parker for the presidency in 1904; almost unanimously they supported Mr. Taft for the Republican nomination this year; the large majority are now supporting Professor Wilson for the election. Some of them still prefer Mr. Taft to Mr. Wilson, but all make either Mr. Taft or Mr. Wilson their first choice; and one of the ludicrous features of the campaign is that those papers supporting Professor Wilson show the most jealous partisanship for Mr. Taft whenever they think his interests are jeopardized by the Progressive movement—that, for instance, any electors will obey the will of the majority of the Republican voters at the primaries, and vote for me instead of obeying the will of the Messrs. Barnes-Penrose-Guggenheim combination by voting for Mr. Taft. No better proof can be given than this of the fact that the fundamental concern of the privileged interests is to beat the new party. Some of them would rather beat it with Mr. Wilson; others would rather beat it with Mr. Taft; but the difference between Mr. Wilson and Mr. Taft they consider as trivial, as a mere matter of personal preference. Their real fight is for either, as against the Progressives. They represent the allied reactionaries of the country, and they are against the new party because to their unerring vision it is evident that the real danger to privilege comes from the new party, and from the new party alone. The men who presided over the Baltimore and the Chicago conventions, and the great bosses who controlled the two conventions, Mr. Root and Mr. Parker, Mr. Barnes and Mr. Murphy, Mr. Penrose and Mr. Taggart, Mr. Guggenheim and Mr. Sullivan, differ from one another of course on certain points. But these are the differences which one corporation lawyer has with another corporation lawyer when acting for different corporations. They come together at once as against a common enemy when the dominion of both is threatened by the supremacy of the people of the United States, now aroused to the need of a national alignment on the vital economic issues of this generation.

Neither the Republican nor the Democratic platform contains the slightest promise of approaching the great problems of today either with understanding or good faith; and yet never was there greater need in this nation than now of understanding and of action taken in good faith, on the part of the men and the organizations shaping our governmental policy. Moreover, our needs are such that there should be coherent action among those responsible for the conduct of national affairs and those responsible for the conduct of State affairs; because our aim should be the same in both State and nation; that is, to use the government as an efficient agency for the practical betterment of social and economic conditions throughout this land. There are other important things to be done, but this is the most important thing. It is preposterous to leave such a movement in the hands of men who have broken their promises as have the present heads of the Republican organization (not of the Republican voters, for they in no shape represent the rank and file of the Republican voters). These men by their deeds give the lie to their words. There is no health in them, and they cannot be trusted. But the Democratic party is just as little to be trusted. The Underwood-Fitzgerald combination in the House of Representatives has shown that it cannot safely be trusted to maintain the interests of this country abroad or to represent the interests of the plain people at home. The control of the various State bosses in the State organizations has been strengthened by the action at Baltimore; and scant indeed would be the use of exchanging the whips of Messrs. Barnes, Penrose, and Guggenheim for the scorpions of Messrs. Murphy, Taggart, and Sullivan. Finally, the Democratic platform not only shows an utter failure to understand either present conditions or the means of making these conditions better but also a reckless willingness to try to attract various sections of the electorate by making mutually incompatible promises which there is not the slightest intention of redeeming, and which, if redeemed, would result in sheer ruin. Far-seeing patriots should turn scornfully from men who seek power on a platform which with exquisite nicety combines silly inability to understand the national needs and dishonest insincerity in promising conflicting and impossible remedies.

If this country is really to go forward along the path of social and economic justice, there must be a new party of nation-wide and non-sectional principles, a party where the titular national chiefs and the real State leaders shall be in genuine accord, a party in whose counsels the people shall be supreme, a party that shall represent in the nation and the several States alike the same cause, the cause of human rights and of governmental efficiency. At present both the old parties are controlled by professional politicians in the interests of the privileged classes, and apparently each has set up as its ideal of business and political development a government by financial despotism tempered by make-believe political assassination. Democrat and Republican alike, they represent government of the needy many by professional politicians in the interests of the rich few. This is class government, and class government of a peculiarly unwholesome kind.

It seems to me, therefore, that the time is ripe, and over-ripe, for a genuine Progressive movement, nation-wide and justice-loving,

sprung from and responsible to the people themselves, and sun-
dered by a great gulf from both of the old party organizations, while
representing all that is best in the hopes, beliefs, and aspirations
of the plain people who make up the immense majority of the
rank and file of both the old parties.

The first essential in the Progressive program is the right of the
people to rule. But a few months ago our opponents were assuring
us with insincere clamor that it was absurd for us to talk about desiring that the people should rule, because, as a matter of fact, the
people actually do rule. Since that time the actions of the Chicago
Convention, and to an only less degree of the Baltimore Convention,
have shown in striking fashion how little the people do rule under
our present conditions.

We should provide by national law for presidential primaries. We
should provide for the election of United States senators by popular
vote. We should provide for a short ballot; nothing makes it harder
for the people to control their public servants than to force them to
vote for so many officials that they cannot really keep track of any
one of them, so that each becomes indistinguishable in the crowd
around him. There must be stringent and efficient corrupt-practices
acts, applying to the primaries as well as the elections; and there
should be publicity of campaign contributions during the campaign.

We should provide throughout this Union for giving the people in
every State the real right to rule themselves, and really and not
nominally to control their public servants and their agencies for
doing the public business; an incident of this being giving the people the right themselves to do this public business if they find it
impossible to get what they desire through the existing agencies. I
do not attempt to dogmatize as to the machinery by which this end
should be achieved. In each community it must be shaped so as to
correspond not merely with the needs but with the customs and
ways of thought of that community, and no community has a right
to dictate to any other in this matter. But wherever representative
government has in actual fact become non-representative there the
people should secure to themselves the initiative, the referendum,
and the recall, doing it in such fashion as to make it evident that
they do not intend to use these instrumentalities wantonly or frequently, but to hold them ready for use in order to correct the

A Confession of Faith

misdeeds or failures of the public servants when it has become evident that these misdeeds and failures cannot be corrected in ordinary and normal fashion. The administrative officer should be given full power, for otherwise he cannot do well the people's work; and the people should be given full power over him.

I do not mean that we shall abandon representative government; on the contrary, I mean that we shall devise methods by which our government shall become really representative. To use such measures as the initiative, referendum, and recall indiscriminately and promiscuously on all kinds of occasions would undoubtedly cause disaster; but events have shown that at present our institutions are not representative—at any rate in many States, and sometimes in the nation—and that we cannot wisely afford to let this condition of things remain longer uncorrected. We have permitted the growing up of a breed of politicians who, sometimes for improper political purposes, sometimes as a means of serving the great special interests of privilege which stand behind them, twist so-called representative institutions into a means of thwarting instead of expressing the deliberate and well-thought-out judgment of the people as a whole. This cannot be permitted. We choose our representatives for two purposes. In the first place, we choose them with the desire that, as experts, they shall study certain matters with which we, the people as a whole, cannot be intimately acquainted, and that as regards these matters they shall formulate a policy for our betterment. Even as regards such a policy, and the actions taken thereunder, we ourselves should have the right ultimately to vote our disapproval of it, if we feel such disapproval. But, in the next place, our representatives are chosen to carry out certain policies as to which we have definitely made up our minds, and here we expect them to represent us by doing what we have decided ought to be done. All I desire to do by securing more direct control of the governmental agents and agencies of the people is to give the people the chance to make their representatives really represent them whenever the government becomes misrepresentative instead of representative.

I have not come to this way of thinking from closet study, or as a mere matter of theory; I have been forced to it by a long experience with the actual conditions of our political life. A few years ago, for instance, there was very little demand in this country for presidential primaries. There would have been no demand now if the politicians had really endeavored to carry out the will of the people as regards nominations for President. But, largely under the influence of special privilege in the business world, there have arisen castes of politicians who not only do not represent the people, but who make their bread and butter by thwarting the wishes of the people. This is true of the bosses of both political parties in my own State of New York, and it is just as true of the bosses of one or the other political party in a great many States of the Union. The power of the people must be made supreme within the several party organizations.

In the contest which culminated six weeks ago in this city I speedily found that my chance was at a minimum in any State where I could not get an expression of the people themselves in the primaries. I found that if I could appeal to the rank and file of the Republican voters, I could generally win, whereas, if I had to appeal to the political caste—which includes the most noisy defenders of the old system—I generally lost. Moreover, I found, as a matter of fact, not as a matter of theory, that these politicians habitually and unhesitatingly resort to every species of mean swindling and cheating in order to carry their point. It is because of the general recognition of this fact that the words *politics* and *politicians* have grown to have a sinister meaning throughout this country. The bosses and their agents in the National Republican Convention at Chicago treated political theft as a legitimate political weapon. It is instructive to compare the votes of States where there were open primaries and the votes of States where there were not. In Illinois, Pennsylvania, and Ohio we had direct primaries, and the Taft machine was beaten two to one. Between and bordering on these States were Michigan, Indiana, and Kentucky. In these States we could not get direct primaries, and the politicians elected two delegates to our one. In the first three States the contests were absolutely open, absolutely honest. The rank and file expressed their wishes, and there was no taint of fraud about what they did. In the other three States the contest was marked by every species of fraud and violence on the part of our opponents, and half the Taft delegates in the Chicago Convention from these States had tainted titles. The

A Confession of Faith

39

entire Wall Street press at this moment is vigorously engaged in
denouncing the direct primary system and upholding the old convention system, or, as they call it, the "old representative system."
They are so doing because they know that the bosses and the powers of special privilege have tenfold the chance under the convention system that they have when the rank and file of the people can
express themselves at the primaries. The nomination of Mr. Taft at
Chicago was a fraud upon the rank and file of the Republican party;
it was obtained only by defrauding the rank and file of the party of
their right to express their choice; and such fraudulent action does
not bind a single honest member of the party.

Well, what the national committee and the fraudulent majority
of the national convention did at Chicago in misrepresenting the
people has been done again and again in Congress, perhaps especially in the Senate, and in the State legislatures. Again and again
laws demanded by the people have been refused to the people because the representatives of the people misrepresented them.

Now, my proposal is merely that we shall give to the people the
power, to be used not wantonly but only in exceptional cases, themselves to see to it that the governmental action taken in their name
is really the action that they desire.

The American people, and not the courts, are to determine their
own fundamental policies. The people should have power to deal
with the effect of the acts of all their governmental agencies. This
must be extended to include the effects of judicial acts as well as
the acts of the executive and legislative representatives of the people. Where the judge merely does justice as between man and man,
not dealing with constitutional questions, then the interest of the
public is only to see that he is a wise and upright judge. Means
should be devised for making it easier than at present to get rid of
an incompetent judge; means should be devised by the bar and the
bench acting in conjunction with the various legislative bodies to
make justice far more expeditious and more certain than at present.
The stick-in-the-bark legalism, the legalism that subordinates equity
to technicalities, should be recognized as a potent enemy of justice.
But this is not the matter of most concern at the moment. Our prime
concern is that in dealing with the fundamental law of the land, in
assuming finally to interpret it, and therefore finally to make it, the

acts of the courts should be subject to and not above the final control of the people as a whole. I deny that the American people have surrendered to any set of men, no matter what their position or their character, the final right to determine those fundamental questions upon which free self-government ultimately depends. The people themselves must be the ultimate makers of their own Constitution, and where their agents differ in their interpretations of the Constitution the people themselves should be given the chance, after full and deliberate judgment, authoritatively to settle what interpretation it is that their representatives shall thereafter adopt as binding.

Whenever in our constitutional system of government there exist general prohibitions that, as interpreted by the courts, nullify, or may be used to nullify, specific laws passed, and admittedly passed, in the interest of social justice, we are for such immediate law, or amendment to the Constitution, if that be necessary, as will thereafter permit a reference to the people of the public effect of such decision under forms securing full deliberation, to the end that the specific act of the legislative branch of the government thus judicially nullified, and such amendments thereof as come within its scope and purpose, may constitutionally be excepted by vote of the people from the general prohibitions, the same as if that particular act had been expressly excepted when the prohibition was adopted. This will necessitate the establishment of machinery for making much easier of amendment both the National and the several State Constitutions, especially with the view of prompt action on certain judicial decisions—action as specific and limited as that taken by the passage of the Eleventh Amendment to the National Constitution.

We are not in this decrying the courts. That was reserved for the Chicago Convention in its plank respecting impeachment. Impeachment implies the proof of dishonesty. We do not question the general honesty of the courts. But in applying to present-day social conditions the general prohibitions that were intended originally as safeguards to the citizen against the arbitrary power of government in the hands of caste and privilege, these prohibitions have been turned by the courts from safeguards against political and social privilege into barriers against political and social justice and advancement.

Our purpose is not to impugn the courts, but to emancipate them from a position where they stand in the way of social justice; and to emancipate the people, in an orderly way, from the iniquity of enforced submission to a doctrine which would turn constitutional provisions which were intended to favor social justice and advancement into prohibitions against such justice and advancement. . . .

We Progressives stand for the rights of the people. When these rights can best be secured by insistence upon States' rights, then we are for States' rights; when they can best be secured by insistence upon national rights, then we are for national rights. Interstate commerce can be effectively controlled only by the nation. The States cannot control it under the Constitution, and to amend the Constitution by giving them control of it would amount to a dissolution of the government. The worst of the big trusts have always endeavored to keep alive the feeling in favor of having the States themselves, and not the nation, attempt to do this work, because they know that in the long run such effort would be ineffective. There is no surer way to prevent all successful effort to deal with the trusts than to insist that they be dealt with by the States rather than by the Nation, or to create a conflict between the States and the Nation on the subject. The well-meaning ignorant man who advances such a proposition does as much damage as if he were hired by the trusts themselves, for he is playing the game of every big crooked corporation in the country. The only effective way in which to regulate the trusts is through the exercise of the collective power of our people as a whole through the governmental agencies established by the Constitution for this very purpose. Grave injustice is done by the Congress when it fails to give the National Government complete power in this matter; and still graver injustice by the Federal courts when they endeavor in any way to pare down the right of the people collectively to act in this matter as they deem wise; such conduct does itself tend to cause the creation of a twilight zone in which neither the nation nor the States have power. Fortunately, the Federal courts have more and more of recent years tended to adopt the true doctrine, which is that all these matters are to be settled by the people themselves, and that the conscience of the people, and not the preferences of any servants of the people, is to be the standard in deciding what action shall be taken by the people. As Lincoln phrased it: "The [question] of national power and State rights as a principle is no other than the principle of generality and locality. Whatever concerns the whole should be confided to the whole—to the general government; while whatever concerns only the State should be left exclusively to the State."

It is utterly hopeless to attempt to control the trusts merely by the antitrust law, or by any law the same in principle, no matter what the modifications may be in detail. In the first place, these great corporations cannot possibly be controlled merely by a succession of lawsuits. The administrative branch of the government must exercise such control. The preposterous failure of the Commerce Court has shown that only damage comes from the effort to substitute judicial for administrative control of great corporations. In the next place, a loosely drawn law which promises to do everything would reduce business to complete ruin if it were not also so drawn as to accomplish almost nothing.

As construed by the Democratic platform, the antitrust law would, if it could be enforced, abolish all business of any size or any efficiency. The promise thus to apply and construe the law would undoubtedly be broken, but the mere fitful effort thus to apply it would do no good whatever, would accomplish widespread harm, and would bring all trust legislation into contempt. Contrast what has actually been accomplished under the interstate commerce law with what has actually been accomplished under the antitrust law. The first has, on the whole, worked in a highly efficient manner and achieved real and great results; and it promises to achieve even greater results (although I firmly believe that if the power of the commissioners grows greater, it will be necessary to make them and their superior, the President, even more completely responsible to the people for their acts). The second has occasionally done good, has usually accomplished nothing, but generally left the worst conditions wholly unchanged, and has been responsible for a considerable amount of downright and positive evil.

What is needed is the application to all industrial concerns and all cooperating interests engaged in interstate commerce in which there is either monopoly or control of the market of the principles on which we have gone in regulating transportation concerns engaged in such commerce. The antitrust law should be kept on the statute-books and strengthened so as to make it genuinely and thoroughly effective against every big concern tending to monopoly or guilty of antisocial practices. At the same time, a national industrial commission should be created which should have complete power to regulate and control all the great industrial concerns engaged in interstate business—which practically means all of them in this country. This commission should exercise over these industrial concerns like powers to those exercised over the railways by the Interstate Commerce Commission, and over the national banks by the comptroller of the currency, and additional powers if found necessary.

The establishment of such a commission would enable us to punish the individual rather than merely the corporation, just as we now do with banks, where the aim of the government is, not to close the bank, but to bring to justice personally any bank official who has gone wrong.

This commission should deal with all the abuses of the trusts— all the abuses such as those developed by the government suit against the Standard Oil and Tobacco Trusts—as the Interstate Commerce Commission now deals with rebates. It should have complete power to make the capitalization absolutely honest and put a stop to all stock watering.

Such supervision over the issuance of corporate securities would put a stop to exploitation of the people by dishonest capitalists desiring to declare dividends on watered securities, and would open this kind of industrial property to ownership by the people at large. It should have free access to the books of each corporation and power to find out exactly how it treats its employees, its rivals, and the general public. It should have power to compel the unsparing publicity of all the acts of any corporation which goes wrong. The regulation should be primarily under the administrative branch of the government, and not by lawsuit. It should prohibit and effectively punish monopoly achieved through wrong, and also actual wrongs done by industrial corporations which are not monopolies, such as the artificial raising of prices, the artificial restriction on productivity, the elimination of competition by unfair or predatory practices, and the like; leaving industrial organizations free within the limits of fair and honest dealing to promote through the inherent efficiency of organization the power of the United States as a competitive nation among nations, and the greater abundance at home that will come to our people from that power wisely exercised.

Any corporation voluntarily coming under the commission should not be prosecuted under the antitrust law as long as it obeys in good faith the orders of the commission. The commission would be able to interpret in advance, to any honest man asking the interpretation, what he may do and what he may not do in carrying on a legitimate business. Any corporation not coming under the commission should be exposed to prosecution under the antitrust law, and any corporation violating the orders of the commission should also at once become exposed to such prosecution; and when such a prosecution is successful, it should be the duty of the commission to see that the decree of the court is put into effect completely and in good faith, so that the combination is absolutely broken up, and is not allowed to come together again, nor the constituent parts thereof permitted to do business save under the conditions laid down by the commission. This last provision would prevent the repetition of such gross scandals as those attendant upon the present Administration's prosecution of the Standard Oil and the Tobacco Trusts. The Supreme Court of the United States in condemning these two trusts to dissolution used language of unsparing severity concerning their actions. But the decree was carried out in such a manner as to turn into a farce this bitter condemnation of the criminals by the highest court in the country. Not one particle of benefit to the community at large was gained; on the contrary, the prices went up to consumers, independent competitors were placed in greater jeopardy than ever before, and the possessions of the wrongdoers greatly appreciated in value. There never was a more flagrant travesty of justice, never an instance in which wealthy wrongdoers benefited more conspicuously by a law which was supposed to be aimed at them, and which undoubtedly would have brought about severe punishment of less wealthy wrongdoers.

The Progressive proposal is definite. It is practicable. We promise nothing that we cannot carry out. We promise nothing which will jeopardize honest business. We promise adequate control of all big business and the stern suppression of the evils connected with big business, and this promise we can absolutely keep.

Our proposal is to help honest business activity, however extensive, and to see that it is rewarded with fair returns so that there may be no oppression either of businessmen or of the common people. We propose to make it worth while for our business men to develop the most efficient business agencies for use in international trade; for it is to the interest of our whole people that we should do well in international business. But we propose to make those business agencies do complete justice to our own people.

Every dishonest businessman will unquestionably prefer either the program of the Republican convention or the program of the Democratic convention to our proposal, because neither of these programs means nor can mean what it purports to mean. But every honest businessman, big or little, should support the Progressive program, and it is the one and only program which offers real hope to all our people; for it is the one program under which the government can be used with real efficiency to see justice done by the big corporation alike to the wage-earners it employs, to the small rivals with whom it competes, to the investors who purchase its securities, and to the consumers who purchase its products, or to the general public which it ought to serve, as well as to the business man himself.

We favor cooperation in business, and ask only that it be carried on in a spirit of honesty and fairness. We are against crooked business, big or little. We are in favor of honest business, big or little. We propose to penalize conduct and not size. But all very big business, even though honestly conducted, is fraught with such potentiality of menace that there should be thoroughgoing governmental control over it, so that its efficiency in promoting prosperity at home and increasing the power of the nation in international commerce may be maintained, and at the same time fair play insured to the wageworkers, the small business competitors, the investors, and the general public. Wherever it is practicable we propose to preserve competition; but where under modern conditions competition has been eliminated and cannot be successfully restored, then the government must step in and itself supply the needed control on behalf of the people as a whole.

It is imperative to the welfare of our people that we enlarge and extend our foreign commerce. We are preeminently fitted to do this because as a people we have developed high skill in the art of manufacturing; our businessmen are strong executives, strong organizers. In every way possible our Federal Government should cooperate in this important matter. Anyone who has had opportunity to study and observe first-hand Germany's course in this respect must realize that their policy of cooperation between government and business has in comparatively few years made them a leading competitor for the commerce of the world. It should be remembered that they are doing this on a national scale and with large units of business, while the Democrats would have us believe that we should do it with small units of business, which would be controlled not by the National Government but by forty-nine conflicting State sovereignties. Such a policy is utterly out of keeping with the progress of the times and gives our great commercial rivals in Europe—hungry for international markets—golden opportunities of which they are rapidly taking advantage.

I very much wish that legitimate business would no longer permit itself to be frightened by the outcries of illegitimate business into believing that they have any community of interest. Legitimate business ought to understand that its interests are jeopardized when they are confounded with those of illegitimate business; and the latter, whenever threatened with just control, always tries to persuade the former that it also is endangered. As a matter of fact, if legitimate business can only be persuaded to look cool-headedly into our proposition, it is bound to support us. . . .

Now, friends, this is my confession of faith. I have made it rather long because I wish you to know what my deepest convictions are on the great questions of today, so that if you choose to make me your standard-bearer in the fight you shall make your choice understanding exactly how I feel—and if, after hearing me, you think you ought to choose someone else, I shall loyally abide by your choice. The convictions to which I have come have not been arrived at as the result of study in the closet or the library, but from the knowledge I have gained through hard experience during the many years in which, under many and varied conditions, I have striven and toiled with men. I believe in a larger use of the governmental power to help remedy industrial wrongs, because it has been borne in on me by actual experience that without exercise of such power many of the wrongs will go unremedied. I believe in a larger opportunity for the people themselves directly to participate in government and to control their governmental agents, because long experience has taught me that without such control many of their agents will represent them badly. By actual experience in office I have found that, as a rule, I could secure the triumph of the causes in which I most believed, not from the politicians and the men who claim an exceptional right to speak in business and government, but by going over their heads and appealing directly to the people themselves. I am not under the slightest delusion as to any power that during my political career I have at any time possessed. Whatever of power I at any time had, I obtained from the people. I could exercise it only so long as, and to the extent that, the people not merely believed in me, but heartily backed me up. Whatever I did as President I was able to do only because I had the backing of the people. When on any point I did not have that backing, when on any point I differed from the people, it mattered not whether I was right or whether I was wrong, my power vanished. I tried my best to lead the people, to advise them, to tell them what I thought was right; if necessary, I never hesitated to tell them what I thought they ought to hear, even though I thought it would be unpleasant for them to hear it; but I recognized that my task was to try to lead them and not to drive them, to take them into my confidence, to try to show them that I was right, and then loyally and in good faith to accept their decision. I will do anything for the people except what my conscience tells me is wrong, and that I can do for no man and no set of men; I hold that a man cannot serve the people well unless he serves his conscience; but I hold also that where his conscience bids him refuse to do what the people desire, he should not try to continue in office against their will. Our government system should be so shaped that the public servant, when he cannot conscientiously carry out the wishes of the people, shall at their desire leave

his office and not misrepresent them in office; and I hold that the
public servant can by so doing, better than in any other way, serve
both them and his conscience.

Surely there never was a fight better worth making than the one
in which we are engaged. It little matters what befalls any one of
us who for the time being stands in the forefront of the battle. I
hope we shall win, and I believe that if we can wake the people to
what the fight really means we shall win. But, win or lose, we shall
not falter. Whatever fate may at the moment overtake any of us, the
movement itself will not stop. Our cause is based on the eternal
principle of righteousness; and even though we who now lead may
for the time fail, in the end the cause itself shall triumph. Six
weeks ago, here in Chicago, I spoke to the honest representatives
of a convention which was not dominated by honest men; a
convention wherein sat, alas! a majority of men who, with sneering
indifference to every principle of right, so acted as to bring to a
shameful end a party which had been founded over a half-century
ago by men in whose souls burned the fire of lofty endeavor. Now
to you men, who, in your turn, have come together to spend and
be spent in the endless crusade against wrong, to you who face the
future resolute and confident, to you who strive in a spirit of brother-
hood for the betterment of our nation, to you who gird yourselves
for this great new fight in the never-ending warfare for the good of
humankind, I say in closing what in that speech I said in closing:
We stand at Armageddon, and we battle for the Lord.

III ROOSEVELT AS A PRESIDENTIAL REFORMER

Contemporary Judgments

Lincoln Steffens
GOVERNOR ROOSEVELT—AS AN EXPERIMENT

Lincoln Steffens is best known for his muckraking articles which appeared in McClure's Magazine *during Roosevelt's presidency. As editor of* McClure's *and of the* New York Commercial Advertiser, *Steffens was a leading figure in reform journalism. He was attracted to Theodore Roosevelt when Roosevelt became police commissioner of New York In 1895, and he remained a close friend when Roosevelt became governor in 1899. Steffens' article, written in 1900, was remarkably prophetic. He evaluated Roosevelt's political innovations and predicted Boss Tom Platt's successful political coup that later drove Roosevelt out of the state house into what was supposed to be a dead-end job as Vice-President.*

Theodore Roosevelt's career is a practical experiment in politics. He is aiming at success. If he were content to be good, he would not stand out as he does among the honest men who are known in political life, but who for the most part maintain their personal purity by holding aloof and exerting only so much influence as is possible by arousing or directing public opinion. Mr. Roosevelt always has recognized that he had not only to keep clean himself, but to get things done.

He hesitated once when he was an assemblyman. He became a leader in the House during his first term, and he put through several reform laws by forcing or persuading the party to take them up. In a subsequent term he was so influenced by his many Mugwump friends that he stood out alone, with a few followers to fight; just to fight. This lasted only a few weeks, however. He saw that he could accomplish nothing by personifying a universal protest; so in he went again to get things done, to put through all that it was possible to

From J. Lincoln Steffens, "Governor Roosevelt—as an Experiment," from *McClure's,* Vol. XV (June, 1900), pp. 109–112.

force upon his party, and his record in this legislature was a good one.

When he returned from Cuba, the old question arose in no very new form. Should he stand out with the comparatively few so-called independents and fight everything, or should he join with the machine and as Governor do things? I told that story in the May, 1899, number of this magazine; and the decision to accept the regular Republican nomination and make his fight within the party was recounted there with some of the differences which were bound to come between such a man and an organization. The question raised then was, "Would Mr. Roosevelt succeed in doing the right thing always and carrying the organization with him?" The experiment was going on. It is still going on. The first term of his governorship is about over. What is the result? To tell what laws were passed would not signify, from my point of view; that is a matter of mere local interest. It is the success or failure of the man that is significant, because, not alone that he is honest and practical, but because people believe he is honest; and especially the politicians know this. The only man I ever heard question it was a notorious Tammany legislator; this is the way he put it:

"Say, do you know the Governor's got the best lay I ever seen in politics? I don't see why nobody thought of it before. It's dead easy. He just plays the honesty game, and see how it works!"

Thus even he did not really doubt Mr. Roosevelt's honesty. He simply could not rise to a point where he could grasp the idea of sincerity. Life was a game, and honesty was a pretty good trick to play; that was all.

The two years at Albany have been a severe trial. There were no great pieces of legislation up to attract popular enthusiasm and help the Governor carry his will over the machine's. Neither was there any important executive act to give his position the force of public feeling. It was a commonplace term, and the fights were all quiet contests. All the better for the present purpose. They were within the organization, practical politics.

For there were fights. The Governor and the organization clashed with dangerous frequency; and two or three times Mr. Roosevelt and the leaders looked red into one another's faces, lips tight and jaws set, separating as if for good and all. But each time the Governor won, the party leaders submitted, and cooperation was resumed without any unpleasant recollections. Two of these disagreements, or "splits," as they were called, will do here to tell the whole story.

Louis F. Payn was Superintendent of Insurance when Mr. Roosevelt was elected. He was a Republican grown old in the party; a friend of Senator Platt, the State leader, from the days when the Senator was a novice in politics; and he had been appointed by Governor Black, Mr. Roosevelt's Republican predecessor. Mr. Payn had been a lobbyist who did business on a grand scale, but his friends said for him (he never speaks for himself), that no matter what his past had been, his administration of the Department of Insurance was above reproach. He wanted to stay. His term in office expired on January 1, 1900, and he was glad the end came in the middle of Mr. Roosevelt's term, because he would like to have had the stamp of approval which an honest man could put upon the honest end of his life. The man with a past seemed to be really proud of his virtuous present.

The Governor laughed in a merry way he has, and said that Mr. Payn would have to go. Mr. Payn declared he meant to stay. He didn't laugh, and the Governor didn't laugh so much after that. It is known that Roosevelt is a fighter. So is Lou Payn. He is a surly, vindictive man, who knows no limitations. There is a story that Senator Platt tried once to persuade Payn to "let up" on an enemy of theirs. Mr. Platt showed that it was good politics in this case to forgive; the enemy was a man of power in his district. "No, sir," said Payn, "I won't quit on that cuss while he stands above ground." The Senator looked in the angry face, and saw that this was true. "That," he said, "is the reason you are the leader of only a small section of the country, Lou."

Payn fought at first very fairly. A flood of petitions from the insurance companies poured in asking the Governor to retain the superintendent. They all endorsed his official conduct. This did no good. The Governor began to ask men to take Payn's place. Payn saw the leaders. The leaders remonstrated with the Governor, who answered simply that Payn had to go. The Senate would not confirm any successor, was the answer. Payn had the Tammany senators, and he had had personal relations with enough Republican senators to make them stand by him. Very well. The Governor answered that he would name a man whom the Senate could not fail to confirm, an ex-senator or some good party man. This would have been hard on the Senate, but he was told to go ahead. He asked an ex-senator, and the Payn men hustled around for a day; they laughed in their sleeves. The ex-senator declined the nomination. The party was squarely with Payn, who felt safe enough to say to the Governor that, if he would renominate him, "ole Lou Payn" would stand by the Governor when, when—well, when Tom Platt had thrown Teddy Roosevelt over into the ditch.

The Governor sounded the Senate. The Senate was sound for Payn. He spoke plainly to the leaders. They were plainly for Payn. It was a solid front the enemy was showing, but there was one weak place.

All right. The Governor said that if the Senate wouldn't confirm a man in Payn's place, he would wait till the Senate adjourned; then he would bring charges against Payn, and put him on trial. What could he charge? What did he know—"know" meaning prove?

Well, for example—about that time two big Wall Street men were quarreling, and one of them in a huff got some information about a trust company his rival had a remote interest in. The facts had been laid before the Governor. Among the items was a very large loan to Lou Payn by a prominent corporation officer. It appeared that if charges were made against Lou Payn quite a large lot of miscellaneous trouble would be kicked up for many more beside the Superintendent of Insurance.

That was enough. The leaders asked for that list of names the Governor had. He brought it out again, unchanged, and the first man on it was chosen, nominated, confirmed, installed. Mr. Payn said things privately about interminable war, but this fight was won.

The next was less personal and far more important. It brought the Governor into conflict with the corporations, and only very wise men can foresee the end; some of them say it is the end of Roosevelt.

The Governor has a notion that the way to deal with "capital" is to be fair. That was the way also to deal with "labor." That was the best policy with all the big things, as it was with the little things.

"If there should be disaster at the Croton Dam strike," he said one day, when that difficulty was beginning to disturb New York,

"I'd order out the militia in a minute. But I'd sign an employer's liability law, too."

Half an hour later Major-General Roe telegraphed for troops, and he got leave instantly to call out all he needed.

There is in the man contempt for the demagogic cry against capital, and there is in him also a fierce contempt for the dishonesty and grasping selfishness of capitalists. So with labor. He would shoot into a murderous mob with grim satisfaction, just as he stood up for fair play for strikers in New York when he was a police commissioner.

When he was elected Governor, he said privately that no corporation should get a privilege without paying the State for it, and pretty soon he went on to the logical conclusion that all corporations should pay for the privileges they already had. They were not paying their share of the taxes. They paid on their buildings, real estate, cars, trackage, etc., but not for their franchises. Mr. Roosevelt broached the subject of a franchise tax. Objections were raised, but not much was said till the idea appeared in the first draft of the message to the legislature of 1899. Then the organization opposed it strenuously.

Most of the corporations contribute largely to the campaign funds of both political parties in New York. Republicans never offer any anti-capital legislation; the Democrats offer a great deal, and intend none. The Democratic position in the State is well understood. Most of the big Tammany men are interested heavily in the local corporations, and their private secretaries sometimes write the anti-trust, anti-capital planks. This is all part of what our Tammany legislator above quoted would call "the game."

The Republican organization presented some good arguments against the franchise tax paragraph in the Governor's message: the difficulty of finding honest, expert assessors; the lack of standards by which to determine the value of such intangible property; the danger in the future of hateful taxation which would be confiscation. The Governor said these were all matters of skill. He meant to be only just, and he would consult with the corporations about drawing up the bill. But the leaders urged that there was no public demand for such a tax; and that the party had promised nothing of the kind in the platform. To these the Governor replied that it would be all the wiser to legislate in these matters quietly, without arousing any popular excitement like that which had been turning the West upside down, and he thought that a piece of legislation against the abuses of corporations, put through decently in a "capitalist State" of New York's wealth by the Republican party, would be a good example to set to the "crank" States, which, like Tammany, shouted mightily and did nothing, or wanted to hit "money" out of spite, envy, and ignorance.

The difference of opinion grew to a "split." The period of reason was past, and the state of war was declared. For a while it looked as if all legislation and all appointments would be involved. But the organization chose another course. The Governor might present his message if he would, but the legislature should not heed that part of it which advised a franchise-tax law. The message was sent in, and the corporations began to move. They were told by Mr. Roosevelt that they might have a voice, if they wished, in the drawing of the bill. This invitation was public, and it was perfectly understood.

"Yes, I saw it in the paper," said one corporation officer, "but I guess we won't have to see the Governor."

They saw the organization. They had a man at Albany, the regular man, to watch the bill, and it was said that he had a quarter of a million dollars to beat it with. He saw it introduced, referred, "put to sleep." He reported it dead, killed by the organization, so that he did not have to spend a cent.

"I haven't drawn a contract on it," he said, meaning that he had not even promised to pay anything to legislators to vote against it. "It's a dead duck. I listened to the heart of it, and there wasn't a flutter."

The Governor worried a little. He talked a great deal to legislators one by one, two by two. Pretty soon he was cheerful. He talked to the organization about it. Then he was angry. He saw the leaders of the party in the House and Senate. "Orders were orders," they said, and they could do nothing.

One day, toward the end of the session, soon after the watchman in the lobby had given his expert opinion on the state of the bill, the Governor, finding he could not get it out of committee otherwise, sent in a special message. The "steering committee" would have to report it out if that was read. The word flew about from man to man, the message was there at the Speaker's desk; there, too, were the orders. What could be done? Somebody seemed to recall the exact phrasing of the orders.

This somebody tore the message up—an unprecedented piece of audacity; it was worse: it was a political mistake. The cool heads were shocked. Suppose the Governor should appeal to public opinion with his torn message in his hand! The Speaker became ill, and went home for a day. The watchman out in the lobby was in a fine frenzy. Perhaps he was sorry then that he had no contracts drawn. He ran to telephone to New York; he flew back, and began sending page boys to legislators. The sweat rolled off his face and head.

The Governor drew down his upper lip to bite at his mustache, as he does when he is in a rage. Then he saw, as the Assembly leaders had seen, and he laughed. He dictated another message, and had that delivered at the Speaker's desk. The Speaker received it; it was read; it was heeded. The steering committee reported the bill, and both houses passed it; the sweating watchman with his contracts had come to the rescue too late.

This woke up the corporations, and they began to respond to the Governor's invitation to see him. They had suggestions to offer, amendments, but it was too late. The bill was before the Governor, and the legislature had adjourned. It was a ridiculous situation. The usual hearing was given. Some of the corporations had their lawyers on hand to argue their side. Even this was not in vain. They did succeed in persuading the Governor that the bill was imperfect, and should not be signed as it stood. Would he let it drop and have another bill introduced next year? No, he said, with some humor; he could not very well do that. Would he call an extra session? He would consider that. He decided that it would be fair and worth while. Then he need not sign this bill? Well, he thought that, all things considered, he had better sign this bill, so that he would be sure of having something to show when all was over. Moreover, with a franchise law on the books, the amendments to be suggested would probably be more acceptable to him. The extra session was called, a few amendments were adopted, but these changes were so unsatisfactory to the corporations that they are going to fight the law in the highest courts.

What is the result? The organization doesn't like Mr. Roosevelt as Governor, neither does "Lou" Payn, neither do the corporations.

The corporations cannot come out openly to fight him; they have simply served notice on the organization that if he is renominated they will not contribute to campaign funds. But the organization cannot refuse to renominate him, for he has said openly that he wants to finish up his work: levy the franchise tax, see to the amendment, keep in a fair board of assessors, etc. And besides, he has marked the administration as his, so that for the party to fail to honor him again would be to repudiate its own work.

For the politicians the obvious solution of the problem would be to promote him to a place where there would be nothing for him to do but be good. The Vice-Presidency is just the thing. But Mr. Roosevelt wants work, not a soft place; and he would refuse the nomination. But inasmuch as the organizations of all the States are equally interested in getting rid of such a man, the policy would be to work up a wave of popular enthusiasm which should roll up from the West and Southwest a nomination by acclamation in the convention of his party. This he could not refuse, and thus it might seem that the people had shelved the colonel of the Rough Riders in the most dignified and harmless position in the gift of his country. Then everybody could say, "We told you so," for both the theorists and the politicians have said that it is impossible in practical politics to be honest and successful too.

Herbert Croly

THEODORE ROOSEVELT AS A REFORMER

Herbert Croly is the major example of a gifted citizen politicized by the reformist appeal of Theodore Roosevelt's presidency. Croly became a follower of Roosevelt, left his position as an editor, and formulated a political philosophy which encompassed the programs of Roosevelt's presidency. The Promise of American Life (1909), in which this summary of Roosevelt's role as a reformer appeared, both located Roosevelt in history and outlined a course for the future. Although originally influenced by Roosevelt, Croly

From Herbert Croly, *The Promise of American Life* (New York: Macmillan, 1909), pp. 167–171.

went on to structure Roosevelt's pragmatic politics into a cohesive program. In this way he was in turn able to influence Roosevelt, particularly in the campaign for the New Nationalism in 1912.

It is fortunate, consequently, that one reformer can be named whose work has tended to give reform the dignity of a constructive mission. Mr. Theodore Roosevelt's behavior at least is not dictated by negative conception of reform. During the course of an extremely active and varied political career he has, indeed, been all kinds of a reformer. His first appearance in public life, as a member of the Legislature of New York, coincided with an outbreak of dissatisfaction over the charter of New York City; and Mr. Roosevelt's name was identified with the bills which began the revision of that very much revised instrument. Somewhat later, as one of the Federal Commissioners, Mr. Roosevelt made a most useful contribution to the more effective enforcement of the Civil Service Law. Still later, as Police Commissioner of New York City, he had his experience of reform by means of unregenerate instruments and administrative lies. Then, as Governor of the State of New York, he was instrumental in securing the passage of a law taxing franchises as real property and thus faced for the first time and in a preliminary way the many-headed problem of the trusts. Finally, when an accident placed him in the Presidential chair, he consistently used the power of the Federal government and his own influence and popularity for the purpose of regulating the corporations in what he believed to be the public interest. No other American has had anything like so varied and so intimate an acquaintance with the practical work of reform as has Mr. Roosevelt; and when, after more than twenty years of such experience, he adds to the work of administrative reform the additional task of political and economic reconstruction, his originality cannot be considered the result of innocence. Mr. Roosevelt's reconstructive policy does not go very far in purpose or achievement, but limited as it is, it does tend to give the agitation for reform the benefit of a much more positive significance and a much more dignified task.

Mr. Roosevelt has imparted a higher and more positive significance to reform, because throughout his career he has consistently stood for an idea, from which the idea of reform cannot be separated

—namely, the national idea. He has, indeed, been even more of a nationalist than he has a reformer. His most important literary work was a history of the beginning of American national expansion. He has treated all public questions from a vigorous, even from an extreme, national standpoint. No American politician was more eager to assert the national interest against an actual or a possible foreign enemy; and not even William R. Hearst was more resolute to involve his country in a war with Spain. Fortunately, however, his aggressive nationalism did not, like that of so many other statesmen, faint from exhaustion as soon as there were no more foreign enemies to defy. He was the first political leader of the American people to identify the national principle with an ideal of reform. He was the first to realize that an American statesman could no longer really represent the national interest without becoming a reformer. Mr. Grover Cleveland showed a glimmering of the necessity of this affiliation; but he could not carry it far, because, as a sincere traditional Democrat, he could not reach a clear understanding of the meaning either of reform or of nationality. Mr. Roosevelt, however, divined that an American statesman who eschewed or evaded the work of reform came inevitably to represent either special and local interests or else a merely Bourbon political tradition, and in this way was disqualified for genuinely national service. He divined that the national principle involved a continual process of internal reformation; and that the reforming idea implied the necessity of more efficient national organization. Consequently, when he became President of the United States and the official representative of the national interest of the country, he attained finally his proper sphere of action. He immediately began the salutary and indispensable work of nationalizing the reform movement.

The nationalization of reform endowed the movement with new vitality and meaning. What Mr. Roosevelt really did was to revive the Hamiltonian ideal of constructive national legislation. During the whole of the nineteenth century that ideal, while by no means dead, was disabled by associations and conditions from active and efficient service. Not until the end of the Spanish War was a condition of public feeling created, which made it possible to revive Hamiltonianism. That war and its resulting policy of extraterritorial expansion, so far from hindering the process of domestic amelioration, availed, from the sheer force of the national aspirations it aroused, to give a tremendous impulse to the work of national reform. It made Americans more sensitive to a national idea and more conscious of their national responsibilities, and it indirectly helped to place in the Presidential chair the man who, as I have said, represented both the national idea and the spirit of reform. The sincere and intelligent combination of those two ideas is bound to issue in the Hamiltonian practice of constructive national legislation.

Of course Theodore Roosevelt is Hamiltonian with a difference. Hamilton's fatal error consisted in his attempt to make the Federal organization not merely the effective engine of the national interest, but also a bulwark against the rising tide of democracy. The new Federalism or rather new Nationalism is not in any way inimical to democracy. On the contrary, not only does Mr. Roosevelt believe himself to be an unimpeachable democrat in theory, but he has given his fellow-countrymen a useful example of the way in which a college-bred and a well-to-do man can become by somewhat forcible means a good practical democrat. The whole tendency of his program is to give a democratic meaning and purpose to the Hamiltonian tradition and method. He proposes to use the power and the resources of the Federal government for the purpose of making his countrymen a more complete democracy in organization and practice; but he does not make these proposals, as Mr. Bryan does, gingerly and with a bad conscience. He makes them with a frank and full confidence in an efficient national organization as the necessary agent of the national interest and purpose. He has completely abandoned that part of the traditional democratic creed which tends to regard the assumption by the government of responsibility, and its endowment with power adequate to the responsibility as inherently dangerous and undemocratic. He realizes that any efficiency of organization and delegation of power which is necessary to the promotion of the American national interest must be helpful to democracy. More than any other American political leader, except Lincoln, his devotion both to the national and to the democratic ideas is thorough-going and absolute.

As the founder of a new national democracy, then, his influence and his work have tended to emancipate American democracy from its Jeffersonian bondage. They have tended to give a new meaning to popular government by endowing it with larger powers, more positive responsibilities, and a better faith in human excellence. Jefferson believed theoretically in human goodness, but in actual practice his faith in human nature was exceedingly restricted. Just as the older aristocratic theory had been to justify hereditary political leadership by considering the ordinary man as necessarily irresponsible and incapable, so the early French democrats, and Jefferson after them, made faith in the people equivalent to a profound suspicion of responsible official leadership. Exceptional power merely offered exceptional opportunities for abuse. He refused, as far as he could, to endow special men, even when chosen by the people, with any opportunity to promote the public welfare proportionate to their abilities. So far as his influence has prevailed the government of the country was organized on the basis of a cordial distrust of the man of exceptional competence, training, or independence as a public official. To the present day this distrust remains the sign by which the demoralizing influence of the Jeffersonian democratic creed is most plainly to be traced. So far as it continues to be influential it destroys one necessary condition of responsible and efficient government, and it is bound to paralyze any attempt to make the national organization adequate to the promotion of the national interest. Mr. Roosevelt has exhibited his genuinely national spirit in nothing so clearly as in his endeavor to give to men of special ability, training, and eminence a better opportunity to serve the public. He has not only appointed such men to office, but he has tried to supply them with an administrative machinery which would enable them to use their abilities to the best public advantage; and he has thereby shown a faith in human nature far more edifying and far more genuinely democratic than that of Jefferson or Jackson.

Mr. Roosevelt, however, has still another title to distinction among the brethren of reform. He has not only nationalized the movement, and pointed it in the direction of a better conception of democracy, but he has rallied to its banner the ostensible, if not the very enthusiastic, support of the Republican party. He has restored that party to some sense of its historic position and purpose. As the party which before the War had insisted on making the nation answerable for the solution of the slavery problem, it has inherited the tradition of national responsibility for the national good; but it was rapidly losing all sense of its historic mission, and, like the Whigs, was constantly using its principle and its prestige as a cloak for the aggrandizement of special interests. At its worst it had, indeed, earned some claim on the allegiance of patriotic Americans by its defense of the fiscal system of the country against Mr. Bryan's well-meant but dangerous attack, and by its acceptance after the Spanish War of the responsibilities of extraterritorial expansion; but there was grave danger that its alliance with the "vested" interests would make it unfaithful to its past as the party of responsible national action. It escaped such a fate only by an extremely narrow margin; and the fact that it did escape is due chiefly to the personal influence of Theodore Roosevelt. The Republican party is still very far from being a wholly sincere agent of the national reform interest. Its official leadership is opposed to reform; and it cannot be made to take a single step in advance except under compulsion. But Mr. Roosevelt probably prevented it from drifting into the position of an anti-reform party—which if it had happened would have meant its ruin, and would have damaged the cause of national reform. A Republican party which was untrue to the principle of national responsibility would have no reason for existence; and the Democratic party, as we have seen, cannot become the party of national responsibility without being faithless to its own creed.

Robert M. La Follette

ROOSEVELT AS AN ENEMY OF REFORM

Robert M. La Follette was a rural reformer in the Populist tradition. Elected governor of Wisconsin in 1900 and United States Senator for the first of three terms in 1906, La Follette remained a radical throughout his career. Roosevelt was the first of the modern urban reformers of the twentieth century, and unlike La Follette was always willing to compromise on a critical political issue. This selection reveals the depth of the enmity be-

From Robert M. La Follette, *La Follette's Autobiography: A Personal Narrative of Political Experiences* (Madison; La Follette, 1913), pp. 387–389, 478–485.

tween the two progressives. La Follette believed that when Roosevelt championed progressive causes and then accepted political compromises, he harmed rather than helped the prospects of American reform. La Follette preferred the politics of confrontation to Roosevelt's politics of accommodation, and he regarded compromisers with the same disdain he held for outright political enemies. La Follette resolutely refused to adjust any political stand he took; he felt that eventually public opinion would turn in his favor and help enact his entire program. Roosevelt would settle for any part of his program and hope to gain the rest of it at a later time. The Wisconsin Senator, long a leader in attempts to control the railroads, felt especially bitter about the compromises Roosevelt had made which led to the passage of the Hepburn Bill in 1906.

I state the facts here just as they transpired, because they illustrate the difference in methods which sometimes rendered it impossible for President Roosevelt and myself to cooperate on important legislation. He acted upon the maxim that half a loaf is better than no bread. I believe that half a loaf is fatal whenever it is accepted at the sacrifice of the basic principle sought to be attained. Half a loaf, as a rule, dulls the appetite, and destroys the keenness of interest in attaining the full loaf. A halfway measure never fairly tests the principle and may utterly discredit it. It is certain to weaken, disappoint, and dissipate public interest. Concession and compromise are almost always necessary in legislation, but they call for the most thorough and complete mastery of the principles involved, in order to fix the limit beyond which not one hair's breadth can be yielded.

Roosevelt is the keenest and ablest living interpreter of what I would call the superficial public sentiment of a given time and he is spontaneous in his response to it; but he does not distinguish between that which is a mere surface indication of a sentiment and the building up by a long process of education of a public opinion which is as deep-rooted as life. Had Roosevelt, for example, when he came to consider railroad rate regulation, estimated correctly the value of the public opinion that had been created upon that subject through a space of nine years, he would have known to a certainty that it lay in his power to secure legislation which should effectually control the great transportation companies of the country. But either through a desire to get immediate results, or through a misunderstanding of the really profound depth of that public sentiment, he chose to get what little he could then, rather than to take a temporary defeat and go on fighting at the succeeding session of Congress for legislation that would be fundamentally sound. . . .

Former President Roosevelt, after the expiration of his term of office, absented himself from the country for a period of about fifteen months. It was during this interval that the Progressive movement made its greatest progress nationally. The reason for this is obvious. Taft's openly reactionary course on legislation during the first two sessions of Congress following his inauguration welded together the Progressive strength of the country, and sharpened and clearly defined the issues. While Roosevelt was President, his public utterances through state papers, addresses, and the press were highly colored with rhetorical radicalism. His administrative policies as set forth in his recommendations to Congress were vigorously and picturesquely presented, but characterized by an absence of definite economic conception. One trait was always pronounced. His most savage assault upon special interests was invariably offset with an equally drastic attack upon those who were seeking to reform abuses. These were indiscriminately classed as demagogues and dangerous persons. In this way he sought to win approval, both from the radicals and the conservatives. This cannonading, first in one direction and then in another, filled the air with noise and smoke, which confused and obscured the line of action, but, when the battle cloud drifted by and quiet was restored, it was always a matter of surprise that so little had really been accomplished. Roosevelt is deserving of credit for his appeals made from time to time for higher ethical standards, social decency, and civic honesty. He discussed these matters strikingly and with vigor, investing every utterance with his unique personality. He would seize upon some ancient and accepted precept—as, "Honesty is the best policy"—and treat it with a spirit and energy and in a manner that made him seem almost the original discoverer of the truth. He often confessed, however, a distaste for and lack of interest in economic problems, and his want of definite conception always invited to compromise, retarding or defeating real progress.

It was not strange, therefore, that he approved the Hepburn Rate Bill, and claimed it as an achievement for his administration. For nine years the public had demanded relief from Congress that would restore to the Interstate Commerce Commission some measure of the power of which it had been deprived by a Supreme Court decision in 1897. And, finally, the Hepburn Bill was enacted as a pretended compliance with that public demand. Except for section twenty, which authorized the Commission to enforce upon the railroads a uniform system of bookkeeping, the bill omitted every provision which the Commission had for nine years urged upon Congress as necessary to make the Interstate Commerce Law a workable statute for the protection of the public interest.

Nor was it strange that he approved the Emergency Currency Law—which was but another ragged patch upon our makeshift monetary system, placed there through the powerful influence of the speculative banking interests—and commended it as a "wholesome progressive law."

It was for these reasons that, after a service of seven and one half years as President of the United States, he left no great constructive statute as an enduring record of his service. To the credit of his administration may justly be placed, however, in large measure the more recent progress of the conservation movement. But conservation did not originate with the Roosevelt administration. The Forestry Bureau in the Department of Agriculture was established as a result of a memorial presented by the American Association for the Advancement of Science in 1873, reinforced by another memorial of the Association in 1890. The first national forest reservation was established in 1891. This was the beginning of conservation, which was further promoted by a more elaborate treatment of the subject by the National Academy of Sciences in 1897. Through the publication of a volume entitled "Lands of the Arid West," by Major J. W. Powell, Director of the Geological Survey, and as a result of the foresight and influence of Director Powell, an irrigation division of the United States Geological Survey was established in 1888, and authority conferred upon the Secretary of the Interior to withdraw from private entry reservoir sites and areas of land necessary for irrigation purposes. From this time on the growth of conservation as a governmental policy was commensurate to its great importance to the public. In response to the steadily growing demands, numerous withdrawals of public lands from private sale or entry, for the protection of forests, fuel supply, irrigation, and waterpowers, were made during the Roosevelt administration. In this department of the public service Roosevelt made a distinctly progressive record, due in large degree to the zeal and activity of Chief Forester Pinchot. The enthusiasm of the Chief Forester which led him to include within forest reserves extended areas of purely agricultural lands, thus retarding agricultural development in some of the western states, naturally caused bitterness and hostility to the whole movement on the part of many people in those states whose prosperity depended chiefly upon the development of their agricultural lands. This resulted in building up the only well-grounded opposition to conservation progress. While injustice was done in many cases, the administration of the forestry service has been one of incalculable benefit to the public as a whole.

But the fact remains that the Roosevelt administration came to a close on the fourth of March, 1909, without leaving to its credit a definite Progressive national movement with a clearly defined body of issues. There was the comprehensive and well recognized Progressive movement in Wisconsin. A good beginning had been made in a number of other states, and for three years I had labored in the Senate, making some gain against a solid opposition, but wholly unable to rely on the administration of President Roosevelt for support or cooperation.

On the twenty-fourth of March, 1909, Roosevelt sailed for Africa. He was absent from the country until June, 1910. In that period, under the administration of President Taft, the Progressive Republican movement made greater headway than during the entire Roosevelt administration. This was largely due to the fact that Taft's course was more direct, Roosevelt's devious. Openly denouncing trusts and combinations, Roosevelt made concessions and compromises which tremendously strengthened these special interests. Thus he smeared the issue, but caught the imagination of the younger men of the country by his dash and mock heroics. Taft cooperated with Cannon and Aldrich on legislation. Roosevelt cooperated with Aldrich and Cannon on legislation. Neither President took issue with the reactionary bosses of the Senate upon any legislation of national importance. Taft's talk was generally in line with his legislative policy. Roosevelt's talk was generally at right-angles to his legislative policy. Taft's messages were the more directly reactionary; Roosevelt's the more "progressive." But adhering to his conception of a "square deal," his strongest declarations in the public interest were invariably offset with something comforting for Privilege; every phrase denouncing "bad" trusts was deftly balanced with praise for "good" trusts.

Gifford Pinchot
ROOSEVELT AS AN ADMINISTRATOR

One of the often overlooked strengths of Roosevelt's presidency was his superb administrative skill. Roosevelt was a prodigious reader and an inexhaustible hiker and sportsman. Through his awesome efficiency he managed to do all these things well without slighting the duties of the presidency. Gifford Pinchot served in Roosevelt's administration as Chief Forester and close adviser, and he precipitated the final break with Taft in the Pinchot-Ballinger controversy. He ended a remarkable political career as Governor of Pennsylvania in 1946. In this excerpt from his introduction to a volume in Roosevelt's Works, Pinchot traces the administrative accomplishments of Theodore Roosevelt.

Much of the quality and content of Roosevelt's state papers came directly out of his unsurpassed ability and experience as a public administrator. For while Theodore Roosevelt was the greatest preacher of good morals and good citizenship, he was also the greatest executive of his generation. He led men's thoughts toward sounder views of life and duty and good citizenship. He led also in putting theory into practice—in getting things done.

Roosevelt's achievements as a public administrator have failed of their due share of public appreciation. His powers and his accomplishments in this respect were fully as remarkable as what he did in the field of international statesmanship or as the leader of public thought in America. His management and direction of the govern-

Reprinted by permission of Charles Scribner's Sons from Volume XV, *The Works of Theodore Roosevelt,* pp. xxvii to xxxiii. Copyright 1925 Charles Scribner's Sons.

ment machinery gave evidence of qualities as exceptional as those which made him the unquestioned leader among advocates of personal and civic righteousness.

As a public administrator Roosevelt gave proof of genius in the selection of his assistants, in the formulation of great governmental plans, and in securing a degree of efficiency in the conduct of the public business unmatched either before or since.

The corps of public officials whom Roosevelt drew around him during his presidency was probably without a parallel in the whole history of government administration. They came from every walk of life, and with every sort of background and training. But whether they were public servants already in office when he became President, cowboys, college graduates, frontiersmen, professors, gunmen, writers, scientists, or professional executives, each one was distinguished by intelligent loyalty to the government and to the ideals of the President, and by that combination of devotion to duty and efficiency in service which produces genuine results. Lord Bryce, certainly a competent judge, said of them that he had never in any country seen a more eager, high-minded, and efficient set of public servants, men more useful and more creditable to their country.

Roosevelt used the whole Government of the United States consciously, and with the most conspicuous success, as a means of doing good to the people of this country. The government to him was always a means to an end—never an end in itself—and he made use of it, as he would of any other tool, for the accomplishment of very specific purposes, holding that whatever the people needed, and the law did not specifically forbid, he could do and ought to do.

In his own personal capacity to turn out work Roosevelt stood alone. Nothing, to my mind, illustrates it more completely than the fact that, at the end of years of such effort as would have cost the life of an ordinary man, and in spite of the prodigious rush of the closing weeks, he left the White House with every task accomplished and every letter answered. I was with him when he passed out of its door as President for the last time, and I know.

Roosevelt's undefeated mental endurance made it possible for him to work at high speed and efficiency long after the power to produce at all would have deserted a less hardy and resilient mind. After a day that would have left most men in collapse I have often heard him call for his secretary at ten or eleven o'clock at night and begin the dictation of an important document.

What Roosevelt required of himself he required also, in their degree, of others. In consequence, the actual service rendered to the voters for each dollar of tax expended was immeasurably higher under Roosevelt than under any other of the seven national administrations with which I have been familiar. The driving power of the man at the head; the high and difficult standards which he set for himself; the generosity of his recognition of good work in others; his intimate acquaintance, not simply with the heads of departments, but with the work of subordinates throughout the Government Service; his unequalled power to arouse enthusiasm and command the very best each individual could produce—all these combined to transform, reanimate, and uplift the Government Service until it reached a point of efficiency where, in certain cases at least, government organizations had nothing to fear from comparison with the most effective organizations in the business world.

Roosevelt made it worth while to work for the people of the United States. He was the greatest of public administrators not only because his knowledge of the government was unrivalled, not only because he set in his own person a perfect example of effective work, not only because he was a great master of organization, but because he had the power to establish high ideals of public service, and to inspire in others the same devotion to the public good which illuminated his own life. Roosevelt never said: "Go you and serve the public while I watch you." He said: "Come on, let's do the job together."

For Roosevelt was a leader first of all. The gift of leadership belonged to him in paramount degree. His mind, robust, alert, and bold, led him naturally and inevitably to take the foremost place in every matter with which he had to deal. Among the endless services to his people and his time for which all humanity has profound reason to be grateful, his power to lead supplied, in my judgment, the most essential and the most beneficent.

Knowledge of public opinion, sense of proportion, practical common sense, high daring, and magnetic personality were all developed in Roosevelt to the point that made him the foremost leader of the people of the time in which he lived. Foresight, courage, strength, and skill were not only his as individual characteristics, but they were blended and ripened in the fire of his passion for righteousness until the sum and essence of his whole nature was focussed and expressed in his power to lead. This was the center in which Roosevelt's innumerable qualities and capabilities met and combined. This was the supreme gift which made him the power he was. More than that, it gave him the undying leadership we are still following today.

Leadership implies a following, and a following is impossible, in public life, unless the followers consent to be led. To consent they must be convinced. Beyond any other man of his time, Roosevelt had the capacity of speaking the public judgment on public issues even before it was fully formed. He was continually seizing and expressing in papers, speeches, essays, and articles the public opinion of the American people when it had not yet quite reached the surface—public opinion still in the bud until he brought it to blossom. What he thought today the nation would think tomorrow.

It was this instinctive knowledge of what the rest of the people were thinking, combined with the God-given ability to express it accurately at just the moment when it needed expression, and combined also with his boundless sympathy, that gave the men and women of the nation that feeling of comradeship for him which was the basis of his strength. He felt what they thought, and they knew it was right when he spoke it for them. Roosevelt was the leader of the people because he moved in advance of them, yet never without intimate contact and complete understanding with the great body of his followers.

On our walks together we often discussed this question of leadership, and together developed what we called "the theory of the next step." It was concerned with the fundamental truth that he who goes in advance of public opinion and expects it to follow him must move forward but one step at a time. If his advance is so rapid that the people cannot keep up with him; if they fail to see their way from one foothold to the next; if the gap between the place where they stand now and the place where the leader asks them to stand with him is too broad to be crossed in a single step—contact is broken and the leadership fails.

A leader worth his salt must have courage, for without it the people will despise him. Roosevelt had it to the limit of human endowment. He must have instant perception of an issue and the willingness to grasp it instantly, for otherwise the people will leave him behind. Roosevelt had both. He must have that fine sense of righteousness which sifts the wheat from the chaff and accepts only those things which are eternally right, for otherwise the people eventually will refuse to follow. He must have that mental and moral balance which detects the extremist, rejects the unsound doctrine, and having weighed all things, holds fast that which is good. Finally, he must have the power to speak for the people, to express their thought, to demand that their desire shall be accomplished. He must seize and give voice to their aspiration almost before they are conscious of it themselves.

Roosevelt had all this and more. He never failed to speak his mind, never let the golden moment pass, never left the people without a leader to call forth the best that was in them. The people followed him gladly because he went ever before them on the road which their profoundest convictions declared to be right.

While the people were his friends, during his lifetime Roosevelt's enemies were legion. Today those who question his greatness are few and far between. But Roosevelt wore his greatness with a difference. His size and elevation among his fellow men were not like those of an icy and inaccessible mountain peak, standing rigid and alone among the lesser elevations of common life. Roosevelt was rather like a great plateau, a land higher and more productive than the levels below it, breathing a finer and more stimulating air—altogether a better land—but one where every inhabitant of the lower levels who came to live within its influence might breathe deeper, work better, think higher thoughts, and live a worthier life.

The people loved Roosevelt because he was like them. In him the common qualities were lifted to a higher tension and a greater power, but they were still the same. What he did plain men understood and would have liked to do. To millions he was the image of their better selves.

The people loved him because his thoughts, though loftier, were yet within their reach, and his motives were always clear in their sight. He was larger, stronger, of greater breadth of vision and larger scope, but nevertheless a man whose impulses and achievements, whose sympathies and antagonisms, whose purposes and ideals, were all of like nature with their own. He was like the rest of us, except that there was so much more of him.

No man is great unless his point of view has greatness. Roosevelt's physical and intellectual powers were not without example. I have known a man or two whose memory equalled his; a man or two whose breadth of knowledge might be compared with his; a man or two at least his equal in mental acumen; a man or two the versatility of whose mind did not suffer greatly in contrast with Roosevelt's. But none of us has known a man whose extremely rare endowment of great faculties was at the service of a spirit so gallantly eager to play the whole of a man's part in the world.

John Dewey
THEODORE ROOSEVELT

John Dewey, one of America's greatest philosophers, wrote this obituary on the occasion of Roosevelt's death in 1919. By relating Roosevelt to his era, he tries to explain many of the troubling characteristics of Roosevelt's public career. Dewey pointed out that many of Roosevelt's apparent deficiencies of style and method were actually shrewd assessments of the temper of the time. Without the moral approach, Roosevelt would have been unable to effect any changes in American society. This is an extremely perceptive and well-balanced analysis of the age and the man by one of America's most original thinkers.

In the death of Theodore Roosevelt the America of the generation of 1880 to 1910 lost its typical representative. Indeed, he was its living embodiment rather than its representative. Successful public men are not merely themselves. They are records and gauges of the activities and aspirations of their own day. It is futile to praise them or blame them except as we remember that in so doing we are appraising the time and the people that produced them. Hero worship of the olden type is gone, at least so far as statesmen are concerned. For

From John Dewey, "Theodore Roosevelt" in *The Dial* (February 8, 1919), pp. 115–117.

in a democracy the people admire themselves in the man they make their hero. He is influential with them because he is first influential by them. The ordinary politician is fortunate when by dint of keeping his ear to the ground he can catch and reflect in articulate speech the half-formed sentences of the people. Roosevelt did not have to resort to this undignified posture. He was the phonograph in whose emphatic utterances the people recognized and greeted the collective composition of their individual voices.

To praise or condemn Roosevelt is, then, but to pass judgment on the America which suddenly awakened from the feverish and gigantic expenditures of energy that followed the Civil War to find itself in the face of vast problems and in need of vast reforms. We can better tell the qualities and defects of the period by looking at Roosevelt than in any other way. Through long living in the public eye he had become with extraordinary completeness a public character. It almost seems as if his native individuality, his private traits, disappeared, so wholly did they merge in the public figure. Of every man who goes into political life there gradually grows up a double. This double consists of the acts of the original individual reflected first in the imaginations and then in the desires and acts of other men. Just because Roosevelt's capture of the imagination of his countrymen was so complete, his public double was immense, towering. One cannot think of him except as part of the public scene, performing on the public stage. His ordinary and native acts gained a representative significance. He shook hands with a locomotive engineer, chopped down a tree at Oyster Bay, hunted big game, or wrote a magazine article on his hunting. Each of the acts somehow swelled with an almost ominous import. Each provoked applause or rebuke, enlisting the partisanships of the crowd. In all of these acts he was delightedly *our* Teddy, ours with admiring acclaim or with disgusted irritation. In these acts, almost equally with those of Roosevelt making a stump speech, writing a state paper, taking a canal, or sending a fleet round the world, he was the man in whom we saw our own ideals fulfilled or betrayed. One of the things that rankled most in the minds of those who did not like him was that they could not get rid of him, even in the innermost recesses of their minds. His representative, incarnating force was such that he stayed by them. Everything in American life reminded them of something which Roosevelt had said or done. The assimilation of the private individual with the publicly assumed figure is so complete that for all except his personal intimates the former is non-existent. All that an outsider can say of it is that it must have been great to permit such thorough identification with the public self built up out of impacts upon others, and out of reflections back into the native self of the successes and failures, the applause and dislike of others. Only an individuality at once mediocre and great could have become so wholly a public figure. In thinking of him one is never conscious of mysteries, of unexplored privacies, reticences, and reserves, hidden melancholies, or any touch of inaccessible wistfulness. His inherited advantages of social position, comfortable wealth, education without personal struggle against obstacles, afforded external conditions from which he could launch himself the more easily, without preliminary apprenticeship and without waste of time, upon his task of representing the America of his day. For this America had grown self-conscious about its pioneer days of log-cabin and rail-splitter learning hardly bought by light of candle-dip. It wanted something less sparse and starved, something more opulent, something more obviously prosperous in culture and social standing. It felt the struggles of the earlier day in the scars it had left behind, and rested easily only in the contemplation of a figure which never reminded it of a past which the nation —for so it seemed—had so happily left forever behind. It was a period of the complacent optimism born of success in overcoming obstacles, and of subconscious irritating memories of the shameful limitations involved in having such obstacles to overcome.

Roosevelt was the Man of Action. In that he incarnated his time. He preached the strenuous life and practised what he taught. The age was delirious with activity. It wanted not only action but action done with such a resounding thump and boom that all men should sit up and take notice. Bagehot somewhere remarked that a large part of the avoidable evils of mankind had arisen because a number of men at some important juncture had not been able to sit quietly in a retired room until things had been thought out. The generation had no sympathy with such a notion. If evils existed it was because men did not act promptly and intensely enough. Gordian knots exist only to be cut by the sword of sharp and vehement action. As soon as they are cut, we should have statistics of the number of strands, the variety of snarls, of the size of the sword and the number of foot-pounds in the blow that annihilated the difficulty, Refinements and subtleties and shades of distinction are not for such a period.

To criticize Roosevelt for love of the camera and the headline is childish unless we recognize that in such criticism we are condemn-ing the very conditions of any public success during this period. A period that is devoted to action can have but one measure of suc-cess—that of quantity and extent. This measure is essentially one of social and political reverberations. It cannot be said that it was re-served for Roosevelt to discover the value of publicity for a public man. But he deeply divined the demand for publicity of an emphatic and commanding kind, and he allowed no private modesty to stand in the way of furnishing it. When one has performed a resounding act it is stultifying not to allow it to resound. While other politicians were still trusting to the gumshoe, it took courage as well as genial sagacity to adopt the megaphone. Irritated critics of Roosevelt's ego-tism—which they called megalomania—overlooked the fact that a petty deed cannot be made great by heralding, and that his acts commanded publicity because they were in the first place of a qual-ity to command attention.

Probably nothing in Roosevelt's career so won the attachment of the American people as the fact that he had the courage to take them into his confidence. If it now seems a simple thing for a poli-tician to make the people, in form at least, members of his own household, politically speaking, and to share with them at the break-fast table the political gossip of the day, the simplicity of the per-formance is evidence of the thoroughness with which Roosevelt did his work. He established a tradition which even a man as opposite in temperament as Wilson has felt obliged to follow, and, whatever his practice, to make central in profession. Just as politicians since Lincoln's time have studiously scanned the latter's methods, so fu-ture statesmen will copy the style of publicity which Roosevelt's courageous impetuosity created. Thinking out loud, or at least seem-ing to do so, is one of Roosevelt's permanent contributions to the American political tradition. Lack of occasional spasms of frankness will henceforth be resented as evidence both of lack of courage and lack of trust in the people. And these will become—because of Roosevelt they are already becoming—the cardinal vices to a political democracy. Roosevelt's enemies repeatedly believed that he was politically dead, that he had killed himself. Although the vehemence with which they announced his demise was part of a calculated technique for making their prediction true, they nevertheless sincerely believed that no man could recover from what they took to be stupendous blunders—such as the New Nationalism speech, the recall of judicial decisions, and so on. What they never understood was the admiring affection and unbounded faith with which the American people repaid one who never spoke save to make them sharers in his ideas and to appeal to them as final judges. Because of the power thus given him—combined, of course, with his own power to learn and to grow—probably no public man of any country ever equaled Roosevelt in power to "come back."

Perhaps the best proof of the completeness with which Roosevelt embodied the belief of his generation in action, action unhesitating, untroubled by fine distinctions or over-nice scruples, is the irritation which his personality aroused in academic men. There are a few exceptions, but upon the whole up to the time of the Progressive campaign they followed him with distrust and only, as they felt, from compulsion of circumstances. A mind which apparently never engaged in criticism, certainly never in self-criticism, which in fact identified criticisms with instantaneous assault, was the natural opposite of the mind tangled in the timidities which result from always criticizing, and hence never acting save when external pressure compels.

It would require a history of the life of the United States in the last quarter of the nineteenth century to explain how and why there developed such devoted admiration of action as action, provided only it was on a large scale. But that Roosevelt was a great figure because he was the exponent in word and in personality of this faith there can be no doubt. Nor can it be doubted that power accrued to him because he exemplified his period in thinking and speaking of action exclusively in moral terms. And with Roosevelt as with the type which adores action for its own sake, to think and to speak were synonymous. There are those who think that morality does not enter into action until morality has become a problem—until, that is, the right course to pursue has become uncertain and to be sought for with painful reflection. But by this criterion Roosevelt rarely if ever entered the moral sphere. There is no evidence that he was ever troubled by those brooding questions, those haunting doubts, which never wholly leave a man like Lincoln. Right and wrong were to him as distinctly and completely marked off from one another in every particular case as the blackness of midnight and the noonday glare. Nothing more endeared him to the American people than the engaging candor with which he admitted that in the face of this immense and fixed gulf he was always to be found on the side of righteousness. As he repeatedly confessed, he "stood" for justice, for right, for truth, against injustice, wrong, and falsity. When he did not stand, he fought. Wherever his activities were engaged at all, he saw the combat between the forces of the Lord and of the Devil. The battle at Armageddon was, after all, but the consummating fight in the campaign for Righteousness in which he enlisted when he entered public life. And if upon the whole the moral battle was a cheery thing in which one was stimulated rather than humbled into thoughtful meditation that too reflected the moral simplicity of his generation.

It is true, of course, that the cult of action for its own sake tends to demand for its successful pursuit either a cynical immoralism or the certainty of being on the side of the Lord. No politician in America can be successful beyond the local stage who takes the former course. The good old Anglo-Saxon habit of thinking of politics in moralistic terms was strengthened rather than weakened by its voyage across the Atlantic. Not, however, till the time of Roosevelt were economic problems treated in terms of sin and righteousness. Roosevelt borrowed much from Bryan, but Bryan came from Nazareth in Galilee, and spoke the cruder language of the exhorter and the itinerant revivalist. When Roosevelt uttered like sentiments, his utterances had the color and prestige of a respectable cult and an established Church. It is no part of my intention to appraise what Roosevelt did for our American life in the years around nineteen hundred. But events move rapidly, and if for a time Roosevelt, as the prophet of a new social day, loomed larger than facts justified, it is already easy to underestimate what we owe him. Positively speaking, pitifully little has been done with our industrial inequities and conflicts. But in addition to what Roosevelt did in arresting some of the worst tendencies of the time, he brought men to where they could behold the newer problems. And it is very doubtful if they could have been led to such a place by any other than the moral road, or by any one who did not spontaneously appeal to ethical convictions and enthusiasms. He made the problem of economic readjustment the problem of rebuke of unrighteousness. He endued the cause of the reformer with the glamour of virility and vitality— and all those other terms of romantic energy that come to the lips when Roosevelt is spoken of.

If under the cover of a buoyant and readily vocalized idealism, Mr. Roosevelt took the steps which a "practical man" interested in success would take irrespective of moral considerations, he was in this also the embodiment of his generation of Americans. The generation was not hypocritical—and neither was he. Prosperity is the due reward and recognition of righteousness. Defeat (in that reign of moral law which Americans were brought up to feel all about them) is the sign manual of evil. The cause of righteousness was too precious to be compromised by the danger of defeat; it not only needed to win but it needed the moral sanction that comes from triumph. And Mr. Roosevelt's glory in the fray and his astuteness in discovering the conditions of success blended with his belief in righteousness. He endowed his frequent dickers with machine politicians and compromises with machine politics with a positive moral glow. They were to him proof that he was not as those academic reformers who profess high ideals and accomplish nothing. *His* belief in righteousness was of the sort that "brought things to pass." He trusted—and correctly enough—to a certain ingrained rectitude which would protect him from being compromised beyond a given point; meantime it was the corrupt politicians who took chances, not he. This dualism of theoretical idealism with a too facile pragmatism in action has still to be faced in American life.

When an epoch is closed, the following epoch is not usually generous, or even just, to it. What it achieved is taken for granted; what it failed to do is the outstanding and irritating fact. Roosevelt's period has not wholly passed. The men who fought him are now just beginning to "appreciate" him, and their acclaim mixes with the reverberations from old fights and victories. The fact that the old interests have, in profession at least, moved up to about where Roosevelt stood in his heyday measures the progress made. But it also leaves him by association in a somewhat reactionary light. Above all, men are beginning to realize that our serious economic problems are complicated, not simple; that they have to do with deeply rooted conditions and institutions, not with differences between malefactors of great wealth and benefactors of great virtue; and that for the most part even the most arduous fights of Roosevelt were waged with symptoms rather than with causes. The epoch of "Onward, Christian Soldiers" ended with the Progressive campaign in which it consummated. We are in an epoch of special problems of industrial democracy in farm and shop to which the older idealistic slogans of righteousness and the strenuous life are strangely foreign. Roosevelt's "luck" did not desert him. He has been forever saved from any danger of becoming the figurehead and leader of reactionaries.

Historical Judgments

Matthew Josephson
THE EARLY ROOSEVELT

Josephson is a prolific popular historian who had followed the economic emphasis of Charles Beard. Josephson argues that Roosevelt's power as Governor, President, and reformer was limited and that Roosevelt was adept at playing the politician's game while projecting the image of the complete reformer. In this excerpt dealing with Roosevelt's early years as Governor and President, the comparison of Roosevelt and J. P. Morgan as adversaries and the class analysis of Roosevelt's political appeal are especially noteworthy.

Theodore Roosevelt at forty-three aroused the interest of the country as the youngest President in our history, and one of the most attractive and sympathetic figures who had reached that office in recent decades. He assumed his burdens and dignities cheerfully on the whole, despite the tragic circumstances under which they had been gained. His energetic and informal methods of working, the ease with which he received and dismissed hundreds of visitors every day, his lively sallies, his original turns of speech, all occupied the press and the popular mind. "Every day or two," a correspondent reported, "he rattles the dry bones of precedent and causes sedate Senators and heads of departments to look over their spectacles in consternation." From the outside, Roosevelt's many-sided career now appeared dazzling, meteoric; his personal force, irresistible.

In reality, Roosevelt knew that he was, so to speak, a *captive* President. As at Albany, so at Washington a nearly omnipotent boss, with power to make or ruin him, stood close by. Deferentially Roosevelt invited the boss to hold conferences with him at an early date at Washington; and from Cleveland came Hanna's reply, hinting plainly that the President must wait until he arrived to advise him

From Matthew Josephson, *The President Makers* (New York: Harcourt, Brace, 1940), pp. 117–132. Reprinted by permission of Harold Ober Associates Incorporated. Copyright 1940 and 1968 by Matthew Josephson.

"on many important matters to be considered from a political stand-point. . . ." Meanwhile, Hanna urged, " 'Go slow.' You will be besieged from all sides. . . . *Hear* them all patiently but *reserve* your decision—unless in cases which may require immediate attention. Then if my advice is of importance, Cortelyou [Private Secretary to the President] can reach me over the 'long distance.' "

Roosevelt answered that he would do exactly as advised. He would "go slow."

Indeed from all sides, even by his relatives, he was besieged with the warnings to be cautious, to be "close-mouthed" and conservative. In truth, he understood the situation; and the urgency of these warnings seemed scarcely necessary. To his friend and biographer, Joseph B. Bishop, he confided his intention of avoiding disputes, of seeking to work with the managers of his party, rather than spend his term in strife with them as Grover Cleveland had done.

Moreover, he had felt in honor bound to retain McKinley's Cabinet, even his Private Secretary, Cortelyou, at his side. It was a conservative Cabinet at best; and two of its leading members were old friends and patrons, given to treating him with amused tolerance rather than respect. To the right of him sat Secretary of State John Hay; to the left, Secretary of War Elihu Root. The connections of these men ran straight to the highest circles of Wall Street. Possibly Hay was "one wheel of the old machine of Hanna and Pierpont Morgan, and Root the other," as the old gossip, Henry Adams, surmised.

Another thread which led to the House of Morgan was the appointment by Roosevelt of Robert Bacon, one of the bank's partners, as Assistant Secretary of State—Bacon had been an admired classmate at Harvard. The frequent visits of George W. Perkins, whom Roosevelt had met at Albany, and who was generally charged with handling lobbying and political relations for J. P. Morgan and Company, also pointed to the continued political ascendancy of the great banking house. Perkins wrote frequently from Number 23 Wall Street to the young President whom he warmly liked, giving information of large financial projects in a manner that might commend them to Presidential tolerance. In urgent cases Mr. Perkins would sometimes call the White House on the long-distance telephone.

With regard to legislative matters, as in the preparation of his first message to Congress, Roosevelt went directly to Senator Aldrich's "Philosopher's Club" for advice and approval. "I shall want to see you before I write my message," he told the ancient Senator Allison of Iowa, "because there are two or three points upon which I do not desire to touch, until after consultation with you." Mark Hanna, John Hay, Elihu Root, Aldrich, Allison, O. E. Platt, Robert Bacon, and George W. Perkins—all were consulted in the production of Roosevelt's first, eagerly awaited message to Congress.

Yet, notwithstanding these eminent advisers, Theodore Roosevelt as a young Republican had a contribution of his own to make. He clung tenaciously to those principles he had begun to advocate as Governor. In a confidential letter to his brother-in-law, Douglas Robinson, a New York stock broker who had besought him not to "upset the confidence . . . of the business world," he wrote in very characteristic terms that he intended to propound an attitude of even-handed "righteousness" toward the trusts.

> *I intend to be most conservative, but in the interests of the corporations themselves and above all in the interests of the country, I intend to pursue cautiously, but steadily, the course to which I have been publicly committed . . . and which I am certain is the right course.*

For two years, as we have noted, the great movement toward concentrating industries into single trusts had been absorbing the attention of the country. Then, in the spring of 1901, came the launching of the colossal steel trust, followed by the fierce financial struggle for control of the Northern Pacific Railroad, which terminated in the pooling of the opposing Morgan and Harriman interests in the Northern Securities Company, a $400,000,000 holding company. McKinley himself had noticed, at the time of the Northern Pacific "corner" and panic, the virulence of the trust issue, and according to his official biographer, Olcott, during his second term "reached a firm determination to deal seriously with the evils inseparable from the rapid multiplication of the so-called trusts." Roosevelt had learned that President McKinley had been turning over in his mind what to do in this matter. One often-advocated method of approach would have been to moderate the protective tariff, which was "the mother of trusts." Despite his lifelong championing of protection, McKinley's final public speech at Buffalo proposed a series of reciprocity treaties with various countries for the mutual reduction of tariffs.

Roosevelt in preparing his first message had recourse to this identical solution: reciprocity. But when he broached this point to Senator Nelson Aldrich on October 28, 1901, he was advised to drop the whole business. This the President humbly agreed to do, saying: "All I shall do about the [reciprocity] treaties will be to say I call the attention of the Senate to them." Aldrich was also promised "a last looking over" of the message.

To Hanna, intimately connected with the great oil and steel trades, Roosevelt also turned for advice on the trust question. Hanna wrote:

> *I have been thinking (hard) about that portion of your message regard-ing "Trusts." It seems to me that there are some suggestions which may furnish ammunition to the enemy in a political contest—the question of "overcapitalization" which seemed to have created a doubt in your own mind strikes me as a delicate one.*

The mention of "overcapitalization" Hanna advised him to drop en-tirely, assuring him also that organized labor was in general not opposed to combinations of capital. "They are not worried about the 'Trust' question. . . . Therefore may I suggest that you do not give it so much prominence in your message." Roosevelt had pro-posed some form of enforced publicity and investigation of books; but Hanna remarked, "The inquisition feature is most objectionable. . . . Pardon my suggestions—which have come from careful consid-eration. I see 'dynamite' in it."

Roosevelt thereupon dropped his reflections upon the "overcapi-talization" of the trusts.

True to character, Roosevelt in his first message to Congress did sound, at times, a critical note toward the huge monopolies whose apparition now frightened the average citizen. And this was the dis-tinguishing feature of a very ambitious, long, involved paper, which touched a hundred different topics. He pointed frankly to the evil concerning which others had been silent. He also retained the state-ment that "knowledge of the facts—publicity" should be secured as a means of keeping the trusts a force for good and curbing their "occasional" tendencies to evil. When some of the corporations in their "eagerness to reach great industrial achievements" went too far, the government, he suggested, might inform itself and, while not "prohibiting" or "confining," should in some manner "supervise and regulate."

But modern business was delicate and could easily be thrown out of adjustment, he admitted. "Prosperity can never be created by law alone. . . ." It was not true, he argued, that "the rich were growing richer and the poor poorer." The country continued in an amazingly healthy and flourishing condition, thanks to Republican rule, and nothing must be done to disturb this needlessly.

Such is the gist of an essentially middle-road document that brought welcome relief to the anxious watchers in the counting-houses. It was a performance that ran constantly from "one hand" to the "other hand," as the informal political philosopher, Mr. Dooley, soon noted. Yet to dismiss it as purely opportunist would be to miss its nuances and to differentiate a Theodore Roosevelt in no way from his predecessor McKinley. Though still very moderate, the expression of a spirit critical toward the canons of the respectable can already be observed here. There are also, in references to the new imperial policies, accents of an intense nationalism. But here Roosevelt differs from the older leaders of the Hamiltonian party, who ignored the popular demand for the safeguarding of democratic, equalitarian rights under new forms of attack; he differs from them in seeking to give "a democratic meaning and purpose to the Hamiltonian tradition and method."

Theodore Roosevelt, arriving suddenly in the office of President with its enormous powers under the Constitution, found that he actually held not much real power. Control of the party organization and of parliamentary activities seemed pretty thoroughly vested in Hanna, Aldrich, and a few of their associates. These men with their managerial or pivotal controls, buttressed by vast resources of money, could easily have moved to discredit and crush the unwelcome successor of McKinley, though it would have been a costly business, as in the case of Andrew Johnson. But Roosevelt acted warily, and, at the outset, respected the existing arrangements. He respected the huge, crude strength of Hanna, and the silent, confident force of the more polished Aldrich. How much he deferred to these men and their lieutenants is shown by the disposition of Federal patronage in his first administration—an inescapable sign, since the machinery of their "indirect" rulership rested as always upon the loaves and fishes of office.

To the famous corned-beef-hash breakfasts which Hanna served at the Hotel Arlington in Washington, Roosevelt came frequently for "consultations," just as he had formerly come to Platt's Sunday breakfasts in New York. A stupendous amount of patronage, in the shape of petty appointments, continued to be cleared through Hanna in 1902 and 1903, as is shown by the voluminous private correspondence between the two men. "I see by the papers," runs a characteristic message from Hanna, "that you are thinking of appointing Mr. ——— as ———. Please go slow about this. Will see you tomorrow." Thus the army of Republican "workers," holding post-office, revenue, and lighthouse jobs throughout the country, continued to be provisioned by the national party boss.

In a similar manner Senator Matthew Stanley Quay of Pennsylvania, almost as powerful a boss as Hanna, was freely provided with minor offices. Concerning this old knave, who had been close to the gates of the penitentiary, Roosevelt once remarked, shrugging his shoulders, that it was not his fault if the people of Pennsylvania had elected the man as United States Senator. Also in the Western states, Roosevelt reinforced party orthodoxy against insurgence, by furnishing Henry C. Payne, his Postmaster General—rather than Governor La Follette—with Federal patronage in Wisconsin. Payne, who "represented" public-utility and railroad interests, was a "Standpatter."

In quiet fashion, Roosevelt passed out the desired loaves and fishes to these men who dominated what would later be known as our "invisible government." More publicly, however, he would point with pride to his selection of meritorious and distinguished young administrators to office, wherever possible, for in his heart the Mugwump, the civil-service reformer, still lived. Regarding the administration of the new colonies, where war and danger lurked, he decreed publicly that "no appointments . . . will be dictated or controlled by political considerations."

But Theodore Roosevelt was never made to be a yielding, a complaisant character. Though he found his sphere sharply limited, he could not refrain from pressing instinctively, everywhere, to win more power; and this unremitting process was to end by changing the very traditions surrounding the office of the President.

At Albany he had learned how to carry out "horse trades" even with the wily Tom Platt, winning consent to reformist legislation, and credit for ousting crooked office-holders, in return for concessions to the boss's requirements in other directions. So in Washington, in a series of conferences with the wise old men of the party, the younger politician played a shrewd, determined game for the sake of concessions opening the road for his own ambitions.

A very plausible and appealing theory has been worked out by the late Professor Nathaniel W. Stephenson (based on a study of the Aldrich private papers) that Roosevelt at the outset of his term worked out a truce or "gentleman's agreement" with Hanna and Aldrich, which though circumscribing his field of operations gave him a free hand in certain areas. On August 23, 1902, there was a private gathering of the elder Senators, including Mark Hanna, at Oyster Bay, for an all-day conference. Again, on September 16, 1902, Roosevelt sailed across Long Island Sound to Narragansett, near Newport, where Aldrich's great castle stood, and conferred all day with the gentleman from Rhode Island and his colleagues in the Senate.

The upshot was that the President agreed to leave undisturbed the protective tariff system and the monetary system, those monumental achievements of the Republican party. However, as reports ran, he was "to have his head on all things outside of economics and finance." For instance, Roosevelt might have thought of "Bryanizing" a little. There was now a powerful popular movement for the Eight-Hour Day earnestly pushed by the trade unions and many liberal sympathizers throughout the country. Did Roosevelt agree with Hanna, Aldrich, Cannon, and company to avoid this subject? The idea of the Eight-Hour Day for labor was to spread widely, but without the blessing of the White House, where the counsels of Aldrich, Spooner, Allison, O. H. Platt (of Connecticut), and Mark Hanna were to prevail.

Concerning the whole vague "trust question," which engrossed public opinion, the Republican elders, save for Senator Hanna, showed a certain resignation amounting almost to indifference. Much doubt existed that the government could actually curb the monopolistic corporations under existing laws and court rulings. Moreover, the legal character of the trusts was now being rapidly transformed by clever lawyers into new guises permitted by the New Jersey and Delaware charters. When Roosevelt, soon afterward, opened a government suit against one of the notorious new "holding companies," none of the Aldrich group objected.

Shortly after the second of these conferences, in September, 1902, Roosevelt departed upon a Western tour, and stopping at Logansport, Indiana, made an important "policy" speech touching questions of tariff and finance. Though there was said to be much discontent in the Middle West regarding the tariff and the trusts, he urged the need for continuity in our government revenue laws. To make abrupt changes was dangerous. "What we really need is to treat the tariff as a business proposition," he declared, "and not from the standpoint of a political party." The nation could adjust its business to a given tariff schedule. But changes should be managed by experts, working "primarily from the standpoint of the business interests."

The philosophers of the Senate, both Allison and Spooner, at once wrote Roosevelt that his were brave words, "sound and wise . . . will do much to clear the atmosphere." They concluded: "Have done immeasurable good." And he replied (to Allison): "I thought I had substantially the idea that we agreed upon at the time you were in Oyster Bay."

Roosevelt in short was not to disturb the economic legislation which favored industrial capitalism, nor the financial policy, the gold standard, favored by the Eastern bankers. In truth he was never highly interested in these matters, confessing that economic questions were beyond his grasp. But, in compensation, he could pursue freely a "spirited" foreign policy, and he could engage to his heart's content in vigorous but essentially "moral" crusades against the trusts, those "heejeous monsthers," as Mr. Dooley styled them. . . .

As at Albany, so at Washington, Roosevelt studied the popular mood carefully and searched for Live Issues, the ideological raw material of the genuine politician. Nor were they far to seek.

For two years an agitated discussion of the coming of the great trusts was whipped up in the popular press; though it did not reach the intensity of the period between 1904 and 1912, discussion of the trust question was the paramount subject of the Rooseveltian Era. In the Middle West the problem of the high cost of living aroused discontent among an important minority that had always been allied with the Republican party. The high cost of living was widely attributed there to the appearance of the monopolies in steel, nails, barbed wire, shoes, wool, tobacco, all the consumer goods which the farmer must purchase. In the usually safe State of Iowa, the rise of Albert Cummins as a dominant political leader, toward 1901, was a symptom; Cummins, though a Republican, preached tariff reduction as a measure with which to combat the trusts. In Wisconsin, where the radical La Follette now ruled, a strong anti-railroad movement flourished. And in Minnesota the merging of the two competing trunk lines, the Great Northern and Northern Pacific, had led to an attempt at a suit by Governor Van Sant against the parent holding company, the Northern Securities.

Rumblings of protest could be heard by sensitive ears throughout the Mississippi Valley, and especially in the "Granger" states, which so often threatened to quit the orbit of the Republican party. This movement, it was plain to see, Bryan would attempt again to take advantage of. In the winter of 1902, Bryan's followers in Congress, such as Albert S. Burleson of Texas, prepared to open fire upon the new President because of his initial "mildness" toward the big corporations. But though breaches showed themselves here and there in the historic alliance between the Eastern capitalists and the Middle-Western farmers, it is doubtful that Hanna or Aldrich would have moved. They would have continued to "stand pat," while the breach widened.

Roosevelt, however, held different views; and was as confident of the correctness of his judgment as upon the eve of the Spanish-American War. He agreed with Bryan that the trust question was the Live Issue of the day. But in attempting vigorous legal action against the trusts, he alarmed the wise old men of the party far less than if he had struck at the protective tariff.

Not long before this, the railroad bankers, after the violent "Northern Pacific panic" of May, 1901, had composed their quarrel and decided to fling together, by a simple exchange of stock, the assets of three giant trunk lines. This alarmed even men of conservative opinion. A few more such moves on the chessboard of finance capitalism and, as Professor W. Z. Ripley commented at the time, the industries of the nation might be contained within one great holding company, controlled from one banking office, such as that at the corner of Broad and Wall Street in New York. The Northern Securities Company was widely held to be a menacing "Trojan Horse." James J. Hill, who was to be its titular head, admitted afterward that there had been talk of having him manage all of the railroads west of the Mississippi, covering two-thirds of the area of the United States, by means of one great holding company. Even Mark Hanna thought that Hill and Morgan might have gone too far, and McKinley himself would have acted against them in time.

Shortly after his entrance into office, early in February, he asked his Attorney General, Philander C. Knox, who was formerly the attorney of Andrew Carnegie, for an opinion as to the legality of the new railroad holding company, the Northern Securities, whose creation had caused such an outcry. Knox advised that it was a violation of the Sherman Anti-Trust Act of 1890. Whereupon, in absolute confidence, Roosevelt ordered Mr. Knox to prosecute and bring the case to court.

News of the sudden, secretly prepared government action came to financial circles on February 18, 1902, with the effect of the proverbial bombshell. Mr. J. Pierpont Morgan, receiving the news while at dinner, appeared to lose his appetite, and expressed strong resentment at not having been told of the action in advance. Neither Elihu Root nor John Hay had known anything of it.

Three days after the announcement of the government's suit to dissolve the Northern Securities Company, Mr. Morgan, "chaperoned" by Senators Mark Hanna and Chauncey Depew, arrived at the White House to pay a social call upon the new President. Theodore Roosevelt had met Mr. Morgan before and knew him slightly. But the encounter was dramatic.

The one man taciturn, huge, old, craggy and ugly of countenance, was now almost a legendary figure in newspaper prose and caricature, legendary enough to terrify little children. Actually he was not the wealthiest of financiers, but the aggressive leader, heart and soul of the movement of combination in industry and finance, omnipotent in his control of affiliated banks and trust companies, seemingly invincible in his gigantic promotions. The movement he led, moreover, was held to be a part of progress and "natural evolution," hence inevitable. Creating ever new masses of debts and securities, huge new areas of capital investment, Morgan accelerated a tremendous credit inflation which wrought for a time a "boundless prosperity." He now stood at the very zenith of his strange, lonely career, as one of the sovereigns of the modern world.

The comparatively youthful, ebullient Roosevelt, on the other hand, was a kind of political adventurer to Mr. Morgan. He had never been in trade, though he sprang from the more comfortable or upper middle class. He had been a writer of books, a sportsman, a soldier, a government official. He occupied, in fact, a middle ground, and had said with conviction in his First Annual Message to Congress: "We are neither for the rich man as such nor the poor man as such; we are for the upright man, rich or poor." He had a thoroughly middle-class fear of labor in its militant moods, and had shown that he would not hesitate to use force against it. But on the other hand he shared a growing resentment and fear also of the mighty industrial overlords, including the one before him, who had accumulated a degree of power that seemed to brook all efforts of government to restrain them. He would soon say: "Of all forms of tyranny, the least attractive and the most vulgar is the tyranny of mere wealth, the tyranny of a plutocracy." The accent here upon vulgarity is not of the proletarian rebel, but of the aristocrat who, aware of the diminished power of his class, nevertheless professes to scorn mere "money-grubbers."

Linked with the aristocratic impulse another impulse could be noted, typical of a large *bureaucratic* class, the men in political or military service in Europe as well as America at this time, who stood outside of commercial life, but often felt bitterly that their devotion and exertions were unjustly overlooked. Roosevelt shared their "moral" conviction that ambitions might be nobly satisfied, not merely by the acquisition of wealth but by a patriotic career in arms, in service, or in directing grand imperial plans for the glory of country and people. In short, no two men could have offered greater contrast than the youthful statesman and the old banker who confronted each other.

At this time there were few men who cared to face the gaze of this fierce old man. Railroad presidents and great bankers habitually avoided debate with "Jupiter" Morgan over his commands. Now Morgan evidently measured the politician and pondered over the possible difficulties he presented, for this politician was unlike others, whom he usually despised. Roosevelt, who had faced death in the Bad Lands of the Dakotas and in Cuba, stood on the precarious ground he had chosen. He was not to be dealt with by a direct approach. Morgan's impulse to violence, expressed in a letter he wrote the President from his hotel that night—a letter never delivered—was in some manner checked by his counselors. The first collision between these two men was less than deadly.

It was probably at a later, less public conference, that day (February 21, 1902) or the day after, that Morgan's complaints at not having been informed in time were heard. It was then that Morgan made his famous, blunt proposal: "If we have done anything wrong, send your man [meaning the Attorney General] to my man [naming his lawyer] and they can fix it up." The President, however, held this to be impossible; while the Attorney General, perhaps simulating the Rooseveltian pugnacity, added that they intended not to "fix it," but to "stop it."

"Are you going to attack my other interests, the Steel Trust and the others?" Morgan asked. To learn of this was the real object of his call.

"Certainly not," replied Roosevelt, "unless we find out that . . . they have done something that we regard as wrong."

After the banker was gone, Roosevelt pointed out to Knox how well "the Wall Street point of view" had been illuminated at this meeting. Mr. Morgan, he reflected, "could not help regarding me as a big rival operator, who either intended to ruin all his interests or else could be induced to come to an agreement to ruin none."

Though it amused the President, there was not a little allegorical truth and keen insight in this notion of Mr. Morgan's. The political man could rise to the force of "a big rival operator," instead of remaining merely a "supple, paid agent" of the capitalist. That the political government might stand "above" the great capitalists, and act as impartial broker between the other great pressure groups, was another question that would wait long for its answer.

Meanwhile the actual outcome of the suit against the Northern

Securities Company waited two years, until March, 1904, in the hands
of the Supreme Court, which then issued a dissolution order favorable to the government's contention. The disposition of the company's assets, controlled by the court, inflicted no serious punishment
upon the monopolists. Jim Hill, who angrily called Theodore Roosevelt "a political adventurer" and a poseur, vowed in 1902 that the
purposes of the railway magnates would be met "in another way."
Two certificates of stock, printed in different colors, would be issued
instead of one, and that, as Hill remarked derisively, "would consti-
tute the main difference."

The press and public opinion heartily approved of Roosevelt's
suit against Northern Securities—though conservative organs denounced the action. Joseph Pulitzer, the owner of the independent,
Democratic *World,* though personally hostile to Roosevelt, supported
him at this time, on the ground that his actions appeased the masses
of people. "The greatest breeder of discontent and socialism," wrote
Pulitzer to his editor Frank Cobb, "is the . . . popular belief that the
law is one thing for the rich and another for the poor."

It was with the purpose of contending against such dangerous
counsels of despair as Pulitzer alluded to, that Roosevelt, in the late
summer of 1902, took the stump in a speaking tour of New England
and the Middle West. In explaining and defending his action, which
had roused up a spirited controversy, he argued that the trust question was essentially a *moral* question, and that he endeavored but to
deal with it righteously. It was inevitable, with his half-aristocratic,
half-bureaucratic outlook (detached from the economic motives of
both the House of Morgan and the American Federation of Labor),
that he should seek a synthesis emphasizing "the superiority of the
moral to the material."

"Material prosperity without the moral lift toward righteousness,"
left to its own devices, he said, would bring but unhappiness and
degradation to our country.

He prophesied dangers to come from the jealousy of the classes.

> Not only do the wicked flourish, when the times are such that most
> men flourish, but what is worse, the spirit of envy and jealousy and
> hatred springs up in the breasts of those who, though they may be doing
> fairly well themselves, yet see others who are no more deserving, doing
> far better.

Finally, Roosevelt argued, as one who but opposed the "misuse of property," who would prevent "wrongdoing" lest greater wrongdoing follow:

> *I am far from being against property when I ask that the question of the trusts be taken up. I am acting in the most conservative sense in property's interest. . . . Because* when you can make it evident that all men, big and small alike, have to obey the law, you are putting the safeguard of law around all men.

Roosevelt's words were timely; they came at a moment when the bright noon of McKinleyan prosperity sensibly declined; though business activity remained high, the distinctly higher cost of living began now to offset the gains of the four boom years after 1898. Roosevelt's mounting popular strength, however, maintained a unified support for his party among its old followers in the Congressional elections of 1902. His popular strength waxed even greater as a result of the part he played in the great coal miners' strike of that autumn. . . .

John Morton Blum
PRESIDENT, CONGRESS, AND CONTROL

John M. Blum, the associate editor of the collected edition of Roosevelt's letters, wrote several appendices for The Letters *and later amplified them in an important book,* The Republican Roosevelt *(1954). Up to the time of Blum's work, Roosevelt's historical reputation had been in eclipse. The dominant historical opinion, heavily influenced by Henry F. Pringle's* Theodore Roosevelt *(1931), had seen Roosevelt as either a materialistic, power-hungry politician or a neurotic and impulsive adolescent. The appearance of* The Letters *(1951) refuted much of Pringle's psychological portrait. However, not until Blum's book appeared was a case presented showing Roosevelt's positive political accomplishments. The following selection deals wholly with the Hepburn Bill, the first major law to impose effective federal control upon the railroads. Blum argues forcefully that Roosevelt got the best possible bill through a recalcitrant Congress and that, rather than criticizing Roosevelt's half-hearted reform programs, we should applaud his political skill.*

In December 1905, the Fifty-ninth Congress convened. During the fall, the campaigns in Massachusetts and Iowa had kept the tariff issue alive while Roosevelt, in the South, had focused on the railways. The President's annual message, silent, as it had been in 1904, on the tariff, made railroad regulation the central objective of the Administration. In the long struggle that ensued, the tariff once more provided a lever. In the House, a combination of Democrats and Administration Republicans passed a bill reducing the rates on Philippine products. Intended as an instrument of colonial policy, the measure was nevertheless considered by standpat Republicans to breach the principle of protection. Administration leaders in the Senate by their lassitude permitted it to die in committee while, like Roosevelt, they concentrated their energy and their power on the railroad bill. For this division of labor no explicit bargain need have been made, for all matters pertaining to the tariff continued in 1906 to be, as they had been since 1904, useful whips rather than real targets. By 1906 Roosevelt had abandoned all effort for tariff revision, yet essentially he abandoned only a bargaining instrument. At no time in his long public career did tariff revision much concern him. For eighteen months, however, he employed adroitly the specter of tariff agitation.

By defining tariff revision as a matter of expediency and railroad regulation as a matter of principle, Roosevelt established his own position. His life, he felt, was a quest for the moral. What he meant by morality was not always clear, but the concept had obvious components. In some cases, that which was moral was that which could be accomplished. Given two paper trusts to bust, Roosevelt had attacked the less offensive but legally vulnerable pool and ignored the more oppressive but legally secure holding company. By this criterion, railroad regulation was in 1904 more moral than tariff revision, for public and political opinion on the railways divided on nonpartisan lines and the Republican party was less committed to the Elkins Act as a line of defense than to the Dingley Act. That which was moral was also often that which was popular. In making a crucial test of the Sherman Antitrust Act, Roosevelt had prosecuted neither the largest nor the most monopolistic holding company. He had chosen, rather, a railroad merger that had been born of a discreditable stockmarket battle, that consisted of units long unpopular with shippers in the areas in which they ran, that had already been challenged by state authorities. Unlike Justice Holmes, Roosevelt wanted to bring the voice of the people to bear on decisions. Showered as they were in 1904 by private and official disclosures of the iniquities of rebates, the evils of Armour, the machinations of Standard Oil, most of the people, particularly middle-class people, were less interested in the tariff than in direct controls of big business, especially the railways.

But Roosevelt's morality was not simply opportunistic. He felt that the central issue of his time pivoted on the control of business because this control determined conduct, and morality was for him a matter of conduct. He feared not the size but the policies of big business. He cared not about profits but about the manner of earning profits. This was the essence of the Square Deal. Roosevelt fought for railroad regulation because it was designed to control process. By his standard, tariff schedules—static matters—were as unimportant as an administrative agency overseeing day-by-day business arrangements was essential.

These dimensions of morality—practicability, popularity, and especially preoccupation with process—characterized Roosevelt's emergent progressivism. They permitted him to yield, when necessary, on details in order to advance his favored measures. They also persuaded him for reasons of policy as well as of tactics to arrange the understanding on tariff revision and railroad regulation that prepared the way for perhaps the most significant legislation of his Presidency.

Railroad rates could not be regulated, however, until Roosevelt, having committed the House to his policy, slowly brought the Senate also into line. In that second task, as in the persuading of the House, he exercised artfully the resources of office and person by which a President can lead Congress, in spite of the separation of powers imposed by the Constitution, to consummate his policies. Roosevelt's impressive ability to work within the structure of government, like his facility in managing the party, depended less on his arresting manner than on his appreciation of the institutions that shaped American political life. Like Edmund Burke, perhaps the greatest of British conservatives, Roosevelt valued the long wash of historical development, sometimes controlled, sometimes accidental, that had given form to the political society in which he lived. Both were wisely careful never to set up a system of their own. Like Burke, Roosevelt delighted in the processes by which political achievement and further institutional development were made possible. Both considered political peace the breathing-time which gave them leisure further to contrive. As he guided his railroad program through the Senate where formidable obstacles blocked his way, Roosevelt needed and took his daily gladness in situations "of power and energy," in government—as Burke described it—"founded on compromise and barter."

Behind all the political manipulation, beneath all the legalistic forensics, the issue was control. Theodore Roosevelt intended that an administrative agency should have the authority to rectify the inequities in the business of transportation. Nelson Aldrich, the resourceful leader of the President's opposition, intended that it should not. Roosevelt demanded that the Interstate Commerce Commission be invested with power to revise railroad rates. Here, he felt, lay the key to control. Aldrich, when he drew his lines, sought to transfer the final decision on rates from the commission to the courts, to leave the judiciary in its traditional, ineffectual, disorderly role of monitor of the price of transportation. President and senator, sensitive always to each other's strength, delighting in the test, came slowly to a crisis.

"I am well aware," Roosevelt stated in his annual message to Congress of 1905, "of the difficulties of the [railroad] legislation that I am suggesting, and of the need of temperate and cautious action in securing it. I should emphatically protest against improperly radical or hasty action . . . [But] the question of transportation lies at the root of all industrial success, and the revolution in transportation which has taken place during the last half-century has been the most important factor in the growth of the new industrial conditions . . . At present the railway is [the highway of commerce] . . . and we must do our best to see that it is kept open to all on equal terms . . . It is far better that it should be managed by private individuals than by the government. But it can only be so managed on condition that justice is done the public . . . What we need to do is to develop an orderly system, and such a system can only come through the gradually increased exercise of the right of efficient government control."

A year earlier Roosevelt had sent Congress only a paragraph on railroad legislation. Now he spelled out the elements of what he considered an orderly system of control. These he had derived from the accumulated findings of the Bureau of Corporations and the Interstate Commerce Commission and from the expert advice of the lawyers and railroad men in his Cabinet. Their recommendations, embodied in the Hepburn Bill with Administration guidance substantially as Roosevelt had announced them, covered every aspect of the railroad problem then recognized by the foremost authority on railroad economics in the United States. Grounded as it was on thorough study by essentially conservative men, much of Roosevelt's program provoked little congressional dissent.

The area of agreement was large. The Elkins Antirebate Act of 1903 had failed utterly to prevent the discriminations it explicitly forbade. Alive to this, and to the public's growing displeasure over the outrageous practices of Armour and Standard Oil, practices as harmful to the railroads as to the competitors of the favored, Congress shared the President's opinion that "all private-car lines, industrial roads, refrigerator charges, and the like should be expressly put under the supervision of the Interstate Commerce Commission . . ." Conscious of the experience of the government in investigating both railways and industrial concerns, Congress, like Roosevelt, had reached the commonsense conclusion that standardized records open to official inspection were a prerequisite for the determination of adequate policies of regulation as well as for the prevention of familiar abuses in corporation management. Congress was also willing, by providing for expeditious action in cases arising under the commerce act, to destroy "the weapon of delay, almost the most formidable weapon in the hands of those whose purpose is to violate the law."*

---

* Without Presidential prodding, the Senate added to the Hepburn Bill two important clauses, one imposing criminal penalties for certain violations, another, more significant, forbidding corporations producing such commodities as coal from owning the railroads that transported them.

Had Roosevelt recommended and Congress agreed to nothing else, these provisions would in themselves have been worthwhile but inadequate achievements. They did not fundamentally alter the existing relationship between the federal government and the railroads. They established no new device of regulation. The restriction of rebates, now strengthened, had earlier existed; the inspection of records, now facilitated, had long since begun; the expedition of trial for suits involving infractions of the Interstate Commerce Act had already been provided for suits arising under the Antitrust Act. Roosevelt's orderly system of efficient government control depended not on these precedents but on an innovation to which many in Congress were still openly hostile. The President proposed that the ICC be given limited authority to make rates. As he carefully defined it, this was his central objective.

Roosevelt took his first and final position on rates in his annual message of 1904. He there considered it "undesirable . . . finally to clothe the commission with general authority to fix railroad rates." "As a fair security to shippers," however, he insisted that "the commission should be vested with the power, where a given rate has been challenged and after full hearing found to be unreasonable, to decide, subject to judicial review, what shall be a reasonable rate to take its place; the ruling of the commission to take effect immediately." The "reasonable rate," Roosevelt implied by his reference to the Supreme Court's interpretation of the Interstate Commerce Act, was to be only a maximum rate. This meaning he made explicit in 1905 when he requested that the commission receive power "to prescribe the limit of rate beyond which it shall not be lawful to go —the maximum reasonable rate, as it is commonly called."

Roosevelt's Attorney General had advised that legislation empowering the commission to set definite rate schedules—the objective of many Democratic and some Western Republican senators— might be declared unconstitutional. "The one thing I do not want," Roosevelt explained to one critic, "is to have a law passed and then declared unconstitutional." Furthermore, he argued, the authority to prescribe a maximum rate, while perhaps short of the ultimate ideal, promised immediate, substantial improvement in existing conditions. "If the Commission has the power to make the maximum rate that which the railroad gives to the most favored shipper, it will speedily become impossible thus to favor any shipper . . ." If, after a test, it should prove inadequate, he would then be willing to try to secure a definite rate proposition. "I believe," he explained to the impatient, "in men who take the next step; not those who theorize about the two-hundredth step."

Roosevelt intended primarily to protect individual shippers from excessive or discriminatory rates. He agreed that the maximum rate provision would afford little remedy for discrimination between commodities or between localities, but such discriminations seemed to him relatively impersonal. He cared less about freight classification and long and short haul differentials because he could not readily associate those matters with a doer of evil and a victim. Discriminations against a small shipper or exorbitant rates the President understood and despised. They were, he was sure, immoral. His interest had also political meaning, for the spokesmen of the shippers' organizations concentrated on the problems that a maximum rate provision could begin to resolve. They neglected to mention, and Roosevelt did not apparently recognize, that no recommendation in the annual messages or provision in the Hepburn Bill prevented shippers or their consignees from passing on rate burdens originating in any discriminatory device to the still unorganized, essentially undiscerning consumers.

The maximum rate proposal, in many respects inadequate, properly labeled so by liberals of the time, nevertheless earned for Roosevelt the opprobrious criticism of a large part of the business community and the tenacious opposition of a near majority of the United States Senate. Modest as the proposal was, it challenged the most cherished prerogative of private management, the most hoary tenet of free private enterprise—the ability freely to make prices. This threat gave Roosevelt a reputation, persisting still among railway executives, of being a scandalous advocate of something closely akin to socialism. A more radical proposition, the President well knew, would have had no chance for success.

Roosevelt had constructed the Hepburn Bill with practiced care. Including as it did just enough to satisfy his purpose, it contained nothing that would alarm the marginal supporters without whom it could not survive. This was the last in a series of calculated tactics by which Roosevelt had prepared the parliamentary environment for

his railroad program. "I have a very strong feeling," he acknowledged, "that it is a President's duty to get on with Congress if he
possibly can, and that it is a reflection upon him if he and Congress
come to a complete break." Avoiding a break, understanding his
situation, he made the powers of his office and the talents of his
person the instruments of viable leadership.

He had begun by trading tariff reform for railroad regulation. He
had continued, after the adjournment of the lame duck session of
the Fifty-eighth Congress, by taking his railroad issue, then the
foremost national political problem, to the people. At the hustings
his vigorous pleading won enthusiastic acclaim. His "plain people,"
for the most part, heard only the voice of their champion. Signifi-
cantly, however, more careful, more cautious listeners, disregarding
his dramatic allusions, at once could ascertain the moderation of his
demands. Roosevelt's message was simple. His demands were not
new. Indeed, Roosevelt added nothing to the principles or to the
histrionics of the Granger and Populist railroad regulators of years
gone by. But he did bring to their long-rejected national program a
new respectability, an incomparable personal vitality, and assur-
ances, impressive to thoughtful conservatives, that he, unlike his
predecessors, would direct regulation to constructive ends.

The last was particularly important. By the fall of 1905 such reliable Republican senators from the West as Allison of Iowa and
Spooner of Wisconsin, traditionally conservators of the status quo,
now sensitive to the growing complaints of the farmers and shippers
whose protests had preceded and exceeded Roosevelt's, realized
that their political life rested upon an unprecedented capitulation to
their constituents. In the President they recognized a safe sponsor
for reform. If his language seemed at times extravagant, if his central
purpose was a genuine departure from the past, he nevertheless,
they knew from experience, guarded their party and, in the largest
sense, their principles. This knowledge may also have comforted
others who deeply distrusted the emotions Roosevelt evoked. Before
the Fifty-ninth Congress convened, the roar of the President's crowds
penetrated, perhaps, the cold quiet where Nelson Aldrich, by preference undisturbed, made policy. That master of the Senate, in any
case, was thereafter willing to make a conciliatory gesture toward
Roosevelt and his allies.

The President had set his stage. Reminded of the arrangements by which the tariff remained inviolate, the new House in February 1906, with only seven adverse votes, passed the Hepburn Bill. It provided for every objective of the Administration. The most thoughtful member of the ICC, Commissioner Prouty, told Roosevelt that it represented "an advance so extraordinary that he had never dared to suppose it would be possible to pass it." The President judged that it was "as far as we could with wisdom go at this time." Politically he was surely correct. Although an aroused constituency cheered the champions of the bill in the Senate, Nelson Aldrich, as debate began, had yet to surrender command of the chamber he had so long dominated. Roosevelt, until this time the aggressor, had now to adjust to the strength and the tactics of a talented oppositionist.

How unlike the President in many ways his adversary was: so urbane, so controlled, so indifferent to manifestations of approval, so patently disdainful of the string-tie statesmanship surrounding him; but, like Roosevelt, so bemused by the endless adventure of governing men! Did his friend Allison have, of a summer, to explain himself in ponderous periods from a rural podium? How dreary for Allison. Aldrich preferred the politics that the caucus controlled, the constituents one met graciously over liqueurs, the measured exchanges between mutually respectful equals who understood the manners and the meaning of their power. For all that, Aldrich was not the less discerning, not the less tenacious. Many of the dreadful things that Theodore did, the senator knew, he had to do. The people, after all, could vote. The railroads were unpopular. Roosevelt could have his bill, but not the way he wanted it. A gesture now, a delaying action—then, perhaps, the worst would pass. Perhaps, again, it would not pass; the comfortable world was changing. In that case, delay had of itself some value. And the means to resist were familiar and strong.

Aldrich had a corps of allies: among the Republicans, the intractables, all reliable, some expert parliamentarians, some outstanding men. There were also among the Democrats those who regularly resisted any reform and others, bound by quixotic tradition confounded with visions of miscegenation, who could be made to shy at any extension of the federal executive power. These were less reliable. Yet Aldrich in the past by prestige and by persuasion had combined these parts into a solid phalanx to front, unbudging, the bills that carried change.

Aldrich, disingenuous, moved quietly to bring the Hepburn Bill with its objectionable clause on rates into the arena where he and his allies had long had their way. While the measure lay before the Committee on Interstate and Foreign Commerce he labored at a disadvantage. There, with few exceptions, his trusted assistants had no seat. There Roosevelt's friends, making the President's moderation their own, seemed capable by cooperation with the Democratic committeemen of carrying crucial votes. There Jonathan Dolliver, the junior senator from Iowa, then beginning the progressive period of his career, ably pleaded the case of the Administration. Dolliver's continuing intimacy with Roosevelt and Attorney General Moody made him as informed as he was ardent. If Dolliver could with the Democrats model the bill to Roosevelt's satisfaction and then bring it out of committee as a party measure, he would have thereafter a tactical advantage. In these parts, Aldrich did not try to shape the bill in committee. He could not have persuaded a majority to go his way, but he could and did persuade a majority to ease his way. Seeming to yield, disarming Dolliver, Aldrich permitted the Hepburn Bill to be reported unamended. Then, supported by Democratic votes on which Dolliver had counted, he secured a motion reserving to each committee member the right to propose amendments from the floor. The issue, still unresolved, was now before the whole Senate.

The same Democratic votes sustained Aldrich's next move. Had Dolliver, as he expected, been designated to guide the measure on the floor, he would still have been an asset to the President and the bill might still have been presented as the party's. Almost the senator from Iowa could see the "Hepburn-Dolliver Act" engraved in history. The Democrats, however, desiring some credit for regulating railroads, preferred that half that title belong to them. This preference Aldrich exploited. He had won the Democrats in the committee to reporting the bill for amendment from the floor by arranging to name as its floor leader one of their party, Benjamin Tillman of South Carolina. With that serpent-tongued agrarian as its guide, the bill could not be labeled "Republican." For Dolliver this was a staggering personal blow; for Aldrich, a beguiling triumph; for Roosevelt, an embarrassing problem in communication. The President and Tillman had long loathed each other. Only recently the senator had made one of his calculated, insulting attacks on Roosevelt's character. For years they had not spoken. Now Aldrich had forced them either to cooperate or to endanger the policy they both espoused. Whatever their course, furthermore, Aldrich had moved the bill into a position where he and his collaborators had an excellent chance of neutralizing it by amendment. "Aldrich," Roosevelt concluded irritably, had "completely lost both his head and his temper." The President had lost the first round.

Well before the Hepburn Bill reached the Senate, Aldrich and his associates had determined on the nature of their attack. Perhaps out of deference to the electorate, they refrained from a direct assault on the maximum rate clause. Instead, they concentrated on amendments by which they intended to endow the judiciary, the least mobile of the branches of government, with the authority to nullify and to delay the rate rulings of the ICC. In behalf of these amendments they debated not the economics of rate-making or the proprieties of privilege, but the constitutionality of the regulatory process, the orderly system that the President proposed to create.

Roosevelt had noted with care that the ICC or a substitute commission "should be made unequivocally administrative." To an administrative body as opposed to an executive department, Congress could, he believed, within the meaning of the Constitution on the separation of powers, delegate the authority to fix maximum rates. This has become a commonplace assumption, the basis of a proliferation of alphabet agencies, but in 1906 men of disinterested conviction as well as those who were sheer obstructionists questioned the legality of combining in one body the quasi-legislative power of determining rates, even maximum rates, the quasi-judicial authority of deciding upon the validity of rates, and the quasi-executive function of investigation and enforcement. The unsuccessful railroad bill of 1905, attempting to resolve this constitutional difficulty, had included a clause, briefly resuscitated in 1910 by the Mann-Elkins Act, establishing a special court of commerce to review the rate decisions of the ICC. The Hepburn Bill as it emerged from the House, however, made no similar provision. Dodging the whole issue of judicial review, it said nothing at all about jurisdiction in cases arising under it.

On the question of judicial review, the proponents and the opponents of Roosevelt's program drew their lines. Contrasted to the large and varied significance of the whole railroad measure, this deployment seems at first almost chicane. Yet since the debates on Hamilton's reports, American legislators had persisted in clothing their differences in constitutional terms. Nor, in the case of the Hepburn Bill, was this lawyers' legacy meaningless. Roosevelt envisioned a new kind of federal executive power to control the complex processes of an industrialized state. He anticipated the methods of the future. His opponents in the Senate, seeking to perpetuate the method or lack of method of the past, relied upon the prevailing dicta of the American courts to prevent the executive from interfering in the day-by-day operations of American business. In government based on law, this was in 1906 still a legal as well as an economic issue. Both sides assiduously spoke the Constitution fair.

The President by no means denied the right of judicial review. He did not believe that any legislation could "prevent . . . an appeal" from a ruling of the ICC. "The courts will retain, and should retain, no matter what the Legislature does," he had asserted, "the power to interfere and upset any action that is confiscatory in its nature." Yet Roosevelt also preferred that judicial review should be limited essentially to procedural questions—to a determination, in any mooted case, of whether the commission's method of reaching the decision had been fair to the carrier. His opponents, on the other hand, hoped to emasculate his program by providing explicitly for broad judicial reinterpretation of the facts of each case. This would have given the courts, considered friendly by the railroads, rather than the commission, which the railroads feared, the real authority over rates.

By its reticence on the matter, the House's version of the Hepburn Bill left to the courts themselves the determination of the scope of review. Roosevelt expressed his satisfaction with this evasion. Attorney General Moody, however, advised him that the measure, in order to pass the test of constitutionality, needed an amendment affirming the right of the railroads to have the courts review the commission's decisions. Roosevelt then considered it only desirable but not essential that the bill provide narrow review. As he began negotiations with the leaders of the Senate, he sought not a limitation to procedural review but only an ambiguous declaration, consonant with the evasion in the unamended version, of the right of review.

Inherent in, but in Roosevelt's opinion subordinate to, the problem of the scope of judicial review was the question of the time at which the rate decisions of the ICC should become effective. Roosevelt had asked that they take effect "immediately," a stipulation the Hepburn Bill fulfilled to his satisfaction by making them effective in thirty days. But if the railroads took to court a decision of the commission, the long process of litigation would postpone indefinitely the application of the revised maximum rate. The House had avoided this problem. In the Senate, while the friends of the railroads wanted just such a delay, the advocates of regulation endeavored to construct some amendment that would prevent the use of injunctions to suspend, pending the outcome of litigation, the rulings of the commission. Roosevelt when debate began preferred, but, as on the question of narrow review, did not insist that the use of injunctions be restricted.

Against the President's moderate, almost uncertain, position the prorailroad senators launched an offensive. Philander Chase Knox, who had while Attorney General seemed to endorse Roosevelt's program, refused in a conference with Moody to reach an agreement on an amendment pertaining to judicial review. Moody's draft, supported by the President, protected the constitutionality of the Hepburn Bill without increasing the appellate jurisdiction of the courts. This was not enough for Knox. In conference he stated that he preferred the House's bill to Moody's amendment. To the Senate he proposed in February that the courts pass on the "lawfulness" of the commission's orders—a term Moody considered so vague as to invite continuing litigation on the economic details and constitutional implications of each rate order. Knox's broad definition of review, carrying as it did the prestige of its author, provided in compelling form precisely the objective of Aldrich and his allies. To graft upon the Hepburn Bill Knox's amendment or one just like it, Aldrich had maneuvered the measure out of committee and onto the floor.

Roosevelt, while Aldrich deployed, had not been idle. From the time the Hepburn Bill reached the Senate, even as it lay in committee, the President had begun to confer with his Republican associates about amendments. Like Aldrich, he had able collaborators. Most helpful of these were William B. Allison of Iowa and John C. Spooner of Wisconsin who, in other years, had with Aldrich and the now deceased O. H. Platt composed the Senate's inner council of control. Allison, of that Four the most sensitive to the tolerances of public opinion and the most skillful negotiator, "rendered," Roosevelt later recalled, "unwearied and invaluable service in the actual, and indispensable, working out of legislative business." Spooner, scarcely less gifted, had a large personal stake in the satisfactory resolution of the problem of regulation, for his home bastion rattled before the guerrillas of the insurgent La Follette. Allison and Spooner brought with them a loyal corps of lesser Western Republican veterans for whom freight rates had assumed pressing political importance. The President could also rely upon, though he would not confide in, the intense Republican left. Could these men clearly demonstrate their strength, others in the party would reluctantly go their way. Finally, there were the Bryan Democrats, Tillman, Bailey of Texas, and a few more cautious in thought and less erratic in deportment who would probably damn Roosevelt's bill but give it their votes.

So positioned, Roosevelt planned at first to carry the bill by sponsoring amendments which would attract the Republican center without alienating the bipartisan left. Throughout February and much of March, while the bill lay in committee, he sought only to perpetuate explicitly the ambiguities implicit in the House's version. The plan seemed feasible so long as the committee might fashion a party measure. But Aldrich's coup, preventing this, also permitted the senator to vitiate Roosevelt's influence with the uncertain. Naturally like Aldrich disposed to trust the judiciary to brake change, the Republican center, relieved of party discipline, now looked more favorably on broad review. Tillman as floor leader for the bill was scarcely fit by temperament or inclination to dissuade them. The President, consequently, had to adjust his strategy to Aldrich's *démarche.*

Roosevelt acted at once. As his personal, unofficial representative in the Senate he selected Allison, who could reach and convince a larger number of Republicans than could have any other possible agent. He arranged also to communicate with Tillman through ex-Senator William E. Chandler, a mutual friend and advocate of regulation. By this clumsy device, with Tillman's help and through Allison's negotiations, Roosevelt then set out to construct a new coalition. "Inasmuch as the Republican leaders have tried to betray me . . . ," he explained, "I am now trying to see if I cannot get . . . [the bill] through in the form I want by the aid of some fifteen or twenty Republicans added to most of the Democrats." For this purpose, involving as it did both the enthusiasm of Tillman and the loyalty of Allison, Roosevelt had to move cautiously but clearly to the left of his original position.

Largely to Allison fell the difficult task of seeking a formula which would solve the problems of judicial review and the use of injunctions to the satisfaction of the divers partners to the potential coalition. Aldrich, if not surprised, must have been a little hurt to find his friend working the other side of the aisle. The work was tedious. Senator after senator contributed to the dozens of amendments under consideration. Three of these sufficiently reveal the nature of Allison's predicament. That of Senator Long of Kansas, the well-advertised product of a White House conference held just at the time Roosevelt decided to rely upon a coalition, prevented, according to the consensus of the Senate, judicial reconsideration of the facts of a case. In endorsing it, the President, no longer equivocal, won the favor of the coalition's Republicans and populist Democrats. Yet this was not enough. Senator Bailey of Texas, Tillman's closest associate, and other persistent Jeffersonians opposed the amendment, as Aldrich expected they would, because it seemed to them an unwarranted extension of executive power. Both Tillman and Bailey, moreover, considered the injunction issue more important than judicial review. The Texan had introduced an amendment, endorsed by most Democrats, which deprived the courts of authority to issue temporary writs suspending rate orders. Although this proposal effectively prevented delay in the application of rate rulings, it seemed to Roosevelt and his harassed lieutenants to be clearly unconstitutional. As negotiations proceeded, the President feared that Aldrich might adopt Bailey's plan or any of several like it in order with Democratic support to write a law that the courts would promptly nullify. Roosevelt and Allison therefore sponsored as an alternative an amendment drafted by Spooner. It provided that whenever a court suspended a rate order the amount in dispute between the carrier and the commission should be placed in escrow pending the outcome of litigation. Spooner's plan at once prevented confiscation of railroad property without due process of law, protected the shippers, and eliminated any advantage for the railroad in seeking litigation simply to cause delay.

Had Roosevelt and Allison been dealing only with resilient men, such ingenuity as Spooner's might, in time, have permitted them to devise a winning compromise. Bailey, for one, began to trim toward Allison. But a few Republicans and Tillman Democrats remained so adamantly for narrow review, many other Democrats so firmly for broad review, that Spooner's promising solution for injunctions never commanded the serious attention of either extreme. Before Allison had a chance to homogenize these stubborn parts, Aldrich precipitated crisis. He, too, had been active across the aisle. On April 18, as he predicted, the Democratic caucus refused to follow Tillman and Bailey. Roosevelt's attempt at coalition had failed.

Aldrich, the second round his, doubtless hoped that Roosevelt would either capitulate or, as he had a few weeks earlier, move further left. The President could have consolidated a noisy defense by throwing in his lot with the La Follette Republicans and Tillman Democrats. He could with them have swelled the rising voices of protest. He might, by such a move, have earned a popularity beyond even that already his. But he would have lost his bill. Seeing this as clearly as did Aldrich, Roosevelt had already prepared once more to redeploy.

Six days earlier, sensing defeat, the President had begun to hedge. If he could not win with Tillman, he might still win on his own original terms without the Democrats. "I am not at all sure," he then wrote Allison, "but that the easy way will be to come right back to the bill as it passed the House, and with very few unimportant amendments to pass it as it stands." On April 22, Roosevelt told Knox, again his confidant, that this opinion was "evidently gaining ground." Indeed it was, for Nelson Aldrich turned toward Roosevelt after the Democrats turned away. The leaders of the

President's Republican opposition by early May ceased to insist on an explicit statement for broad review. Perhaps Aldrich became impatient with the continuing delay in the work of the Senate brought about by the everlasting debate on regulation. Perhaps he decided that Republican solidarity was more important than Roosevelt's purpose was dangerous. Probably, however, he saw that he had miscalculated. When Roosevelt, refusing to list with the left, reverted doggedly to the ambiguous center where he had first stood, he impelled Tillman, La Follette, and their likes, his erstwhile allies, into embittered opposition. Their protestations, couched in their inevitable vocabulary of revolt, attested to the safe reasonableness Roosevelt had ever claimed as his own. The uncertain minds of the wavering Republican center might now hear Allison out—might now, as Allison and Spooner had, see in Roosevelt safety. By some new alignment, like that he had hoped Dolliver would muster, the President with time in *Thermidor* might triumph. At least, so Aldrich may have reasoned. In any case he retreated.

He may also have drafted the amendment which, introduced by Allison, won a majority vote and thereby secured the enactment of the Hepburn Bill. Whether or not Aldrich drafted it, Allison's amendment, leaving the bill in effect as the House had written it, gave Roosevelt what he had started out to get. The authorship of the amendment, like the working of Aldrich's mind, remains obscure. Whoever wrote it, Allison guided it. His activities in the two weeks following the Democratic caucus may be accurately surmised. Leaving no records, the "unwearied and invaluable" senator from Iowa, camped in the cloakroom where he excelled, had fashioned for the President a compromise that satisfied enough Republicans to save the bill.

The Allison amendment covered both judicial review and the use of injunctions. With purposeful obscurity, it granted jurisdiction in cases arising under the Hepburn Act to the circuit courts but left the definition of the scope of review to the courts. In a flood of oratory over the meaning of the amendment, each senator interpreted it to suit himself and his constituents. Both sides claimed victory. Insofar as the amendment was described as a victory for either narrow or broad review, the claims were nonsense. The question of review remained in May as unsettled as it had been in February.

Roosevelt had then asked for no more. Ultimately the Supreme Court, which he trusted so little, in the first decision involving rate rulings made his preference law by refusing to review the facts of the case.

The Allison amendment did affirmatively settle the matter of injunctions by empowering the courts to "enjoin, set aside, annul, or suspend any order" of the ICC. It also prescribed that appeals from the orders of the ICC were to go directly to the Supreme Court with the calendar priorities of antitrust cases. The amendment did not, however, specify the grounds for suspension or establish an escrow scheme. There remained, consequently, the possibility of considerable delay before rate rulings took effect. Roosevelt had constantly expressed his preference for an arrangement less favorable to the railroads, but he had also continually indicated that he would accept a solution like that of the Allison amendment. On this matter Tillman and Bailey, but neither Aldrich nor Roosevelt, had been defeated.

Roosevelt was "entirely satisfied" with the Allison amendment, he pointed out, because he was "entirely satisfied with the Hepburn Bill." The amendment, he informed a less satisfied representative of midwestern shippers, was "only declaratory of what the Hepburn Bill must mean, supposing it to be constitutional . . . I should be glad to get certain [other] amendments . . . ; but they are not vital, and even without them the Hepburn Bill with the Allison amendment contains practically exactly what I have both originally and always since asked for."

Characteristically, Roosevelt overstated his case. "Always since" did not apply, for in his maneuvers of late March and April, although only at that time, the President had asked for more. Tillman and Bailey, who had joined him then, with rankling disappointment attacked him for returning to what he had originally requested. Their attacks, often repeated by their friends, have persuaded two generations that Roosevelt, irresolute and insincere, deserting his friends, yielding to Aldrich, lost the battle for regulation. Surely his detractors felt this, but they erred. Roosevelt had made overtures to Tillman and Bailey only for tactical reasons. He had, temporarily and for parliamentary support, enlarged his earlier demands. When this did not produce sufficient support, he reverted for tactical reasons to his first position. In so doing he deserted his temporary allies, but he did not compromise his policy. Tillman and Bailey, proud veterans of the Senate, perhaps resented most the knowledge that they had been used. Doubtless their pain gave Aldrich, who had made Roosevelt woo them and leave them, some amused satisfaction.

His objective attained, Roosevelt exulted. "No given measure and no given set of measures," he believed, "will work a perfect cure for any serious evil; and the insistence upon having only the perfect cure often results in securing no betterment whatever." The Hepburn Act was not perfect. But, Roosevelt maintained, it represented "the longest step ever yet taken in the direction of solving the railway rate problem." This was a fair assessment. With his clear perception of political situations, Roosevelt had set the highest practicable goal. By his mastery of political devices, in contest with another master, he had reached it. The Senate, in the end, supplied the federal executive with authority beyond any antecedent definition to mitigate the maladjustments of a growing industrial society.

The Hepburn Act endowed the Interstate Commerce Commission with power commensurate with its task. By informed, expert decisions, it could at last alter the artificial configurations of a market that had long since ceased, in the classic sense, to be free. The courts inexpertly had judged transportation by criteria which, however precious in jurisprudence, bore little relation to the economics of the process. Released from the inhibition of judicial reinterpretations (the bond that Aldrich had sought to supply), endowed with weapons the carriers respected, the ICC began to develop after 1906 the techniques of effective supervision. The need for further change of course remained. But the Hepburn Act provided the precedent, accepted by the courts and enlarged by later Congresses, by which federal regulatory agencies have promoted the national welfare. Now vastly ramified, government by administrative commission remains, though somewhat shabby, a useful part of American political arrangements.

For a troubled people in a complex time perhaps only the executive could have become steward. Aldrich, in that case, fought history and Roosevelt only accelerated what no man could have prevented. But Roosevelt's reputation rests securely even in acceleration, for the inevitable sometimes takes too long, and he knew just what he did. His efforts in behalf of the Hepburn Act—a measure meaningful but moderate—demonstrated his skilled concern for creating the instruments he thought the nation needed. For an orderly administrative system, for the right of efficient federal controls, for the positive government of an industrial society, he mobilized in a crucial first skirmish the full powers of his office. And he won.

Only continuous, disinterested administrative action, Roosevelt believed, not intermittent lawsuits or intermittent legislation, not the dicta of the bench or the dicta of partisan and sectional politics, could properly direct the development of American industrial society. This conviction related intimately to his feelings about power and its uses. These in their general implications—both domestic and international—must now be elaborated and explored.

Samuel Hays
ROOSEVELT AND THE CONSERVATION MOVEMENT

Virtually all historians agree that Roosevelt's conservation reforms were genuine and valuable. Until Samuel Hays' excellent study, Conservation and the Gospel of Efficiency *(1959) it was easy to accept the Rooseveltian line that conservation reform simply represented the will of the people as opposed to that of the business interests. Hays shows that conservation, while still central to the problem of Roosevelt's relation to reform, is much more complex than the simple moral view Roosevelt posited. Hays' thesis that efficiency was at the core of much of the progressive reform movement sheds new light upon the moralistic rhetoric that Roosevelt and the progressives used in dealing with everything. Hays' thesis also implies that progressivism may have been more rational and practical than the moral image it tried to project.*

Historians of the progressive era have found it increasingly difficult to categorize Theodore Roosevelt. Was he a "liberal" or an "enlightened conservative"? Did he rob the Democrats of their reform proposals and fulfill the aims of late nineteenth-century social revolt, or did he merely mouth their causes and, in practice, betray them? These questions pose difficulties chiefly because they raise the wrong issues. They assume that the significance of Roosevelt's career lies primarily in its role in the social struggle of the late nineteenth and early twentieth centuries between the business community on the one hand and labor and farm groups on the other. On the contrary, Roosevelt was conspicuously aloof from that social struggle. He refused to become identified with it on either side. He was, in fact, predisposed to reject social conflict, in theory and practice, as the greatest danger in American society. His administration and his social and political views are significant primarily for their attempt to supplant this conflict with a "scientific" approach to social and economic questions.

Roosevelt was profoundly impressed by late nineteenth-century social unrest, and in particular by its more violent manifestations such as the Haymarket riot, the Pullman strike, Coxey's army, and the election of 1896. He viewed Populism as a class struggle which would destroy the nation through internal conflict. He rejected Western Insurgency—a continuation of Populist radicalism, he believed—because it expressed the aims of only one economic group in society which, if dominant, would exercise power as selfishly as did the Eastern business community. The economic struggle slowly evolving from rapid industrial growth aroused Roosevelt's deepest fears. His practical solution to that problem consisted neither of granting dominance to any one group, nor of creating a balance of power among all. In fact, as a result of his fear of conflict he almost denied its reality and tried to evolve concepts and techniques which would, in effect, legislate that conflict out of existence.

Social and economic problems, Roosevelt believed, should be solved, not through power politics, but by experts who would undertake scientific investigations and devise workable solutions. He had an almost unlimited faith in applied science. During his presidency, he repeatedly sought the advice of expert commissions, especially in the field of resource policy, and he looked upon the conservation movement as an attempt to apply this knowledge. But he felt that government could tackle nonresource questions such as labor problems with the same approach. In the fall of 1908 he wrote to a union official:

> Already our Bureau of Labor, for the past twenty years of necessity largely a statistical bureau, is practically a Department of Sociology, aiming not only to secure exact information about industrial conditions but to discover remedies for industrial evils. . . . It is our confident claim . . . that applied science, if carried out according to our program, will succeed in achieving for humanity, above all for the city industrial worker, results even surpassing in value those today in effect on the farm.

Having little appreciation of labor's permanence as a power group in society, Roosevelt believed simply that one could approach the labor problem by improving working conditions, training more efficient employees, and stimulating the industrial machine to prevent unemployment.

President Roosevelt's abiding fear of class struggle led him to conceive of the good society as a classless society, composed, not of organized social groups, but of individuals bound together by personal relationships. Believing that "the line of division in the deeper matters of our citizenship" should "be drawn on the line of conduct," he viewed the fundamentals of social organization as personal moral qualities of honesty, integrity, frugality, loyalty, and "plain dealing between man and man." Thus, he was "predisposed to interpret economic and political problems in terms of moral principles." These moral qualities resided, not in the urban centers, which bred only social disorder, but among the "farmer stock" which possessed "the qualities on which this Nation has had to draw in order to meet every great crisis of the past." Agricultural life was the best means of obtaining that "bodily vigor" which produces "vigor of soul," and independent, property-owning farm families were the major source of social stability and the bulwark against internal conflict. For Roosevelt, with his interest in the out-of-doors, his emphasis on moral vigor arising from struggle with the elements, and his basic fear of social unrest, the good society was agrarian. He would have opposed bitterly any effort to turn back the industrial clock, yet his ultimate scheme of values was firmly rooted in an agrarian social order.

Roosevelt's emphasis on applied science and his conception of the good society as the classless agrarian society were contradictory trends of thought. The one, a faith which looked to the future, accepted wholeheartedly the basic elements of the new technology. The other, essentially backward-looking, longed for the simple agrarian Arcadia which, if it ever existed, could never be revived. He faced two directions at once, accepting the technical requirements of an increasingly organized industrial society, but fearing its social consequences. In this sense, and in this sense alone, Roosevelt sought Jeffersonian ends through Hamiltonian means. He had great respect for both men, each of whom manifested one side of his own contradictory nature. But he admired even more Abraham Lincoln, the spokesman of the "plain people," whose life combined agrarian simplicity and national vigor. By the same token, Roosevelt considered his irrigation program as one of his administration's most important contributions. It expressed in concrete terms his own paradoxical nature: the preservation of American virtues of the past through methods abundantly appropriate to the present.

The contradictory elements of Roosevelt's outlook fused also in an almost mystical approach to the political order best described as "social atomism." Strongly affirming the beneficial role of both expert leadership and the vast mass of humanity, he could not fit into his scheme of things intervening group organization on the middle levels of power. Americans should live, he thought, as individuals rather than as members of "partial" groups, their loyalties should be given not to a class or section but to their national leader. As his administration encountered continued difficulty with Congress, Roosevelt relied more and more on executive commissions, and on action based upon the theory that the executive was the "steward" of the public interest. Feeling that he, rather than Congress, voiced most accurately the popular will, he advocated direct as opposed to representative government. Unable to adjust to a Congress which rejected his gospel of efficiency, Roosevelt took his case to the "people." In doing so he not only bypassed the lawmakers but also defied the group demands of organized American society. Growing ever more resentful of the hindrances of a Congress which expressed these demands, Roosevelt drew closer to a conception of the political organization of society wherein representative government would be minimized, and a strong leader, ruling through vigorous purpose, efficiency, and technology, would derive his support from a direct, personal relationship with the people.

As President, Roosevelt concentrated on problems which would not raise issues of internal social conflict—foreign policy and conservation. Increasingly stressing the conservation program during his second term of office, Roosevelt looked upon it as the most important contribution of his administration in domestic affairs. Conservation gave wide scope to government by experts, to investigation by commissions, to efficiency in planning and execution. It called forth patriotic sentiments which could override internal differences. More efficient production of material goods would help solve the labor problem in the way he thought it could be solved—by providing full employment and lower living costs. Even more important, through the federal irrigation program and the Country Life Movement, both of which Roosevelt encouraged, the President thought that he was buttressing the "Republic" in its most vital spot. Warning President-elect Taft that rural migration to cities would create a decline in the nation's population, in December 1908 Roosevelt urged his successor to formulate a program for country life improvement. "Among the various legacies of trouble which I leave you," he entreated, "there is none to which I more earnestly hope for your thought and care than this."

Herbert Croly's *The Promise of American Life*, written in 1908, articulated these tendencies in Roosevelt's political and social thought. Croly deeply feared that group consciousness in America would lead at best to an aimless, drifting society, and at worst to disastrous internal conflict. Vigorous, national purpose, he argued, should replace the current American faith in automatic evolution toward a better society. Less a blueprint than a simple plea for action, *The Promise of American Life* immediately appealed to Roosevelt as the scholarly expression of the assumptions upon which he had acted as President. And in domestic affairs there was no better illustration of those assumptions than the administration's conservation policies. Croly's work, the President declared, was "the most profound and illuminating study of our national conditions which has appeared for many years."

In holding these attitudes, Roosevelt personally embodied the popular impulses which swung behind the conservation movement during the years of the great crusade. That crusade found its greatest support among the American urban middle class which shrank in fear from the profound social changes being wrought by the technological age. These people looked backward to individualist agrarian ideals, yet they approved social planning as a means to control their main enemy—group struggle for power. A vigorous and purposeful government became the vehicle by which ideals derived from an individualistic society became adjusted to a new collective age. And the conservation movement provided the most far-reaching opportunity to effect that adjustment. Herein lay much of the social and cultural meaning of the movement for progressive resource planning.

Gabriel Kolko

ROOSEVELT AS A REFORMER

Gabriel Kolko is a major New Left historian who, in this excerpt from The Triumph of Conservatism (1963), argues that Roosevelt was a deeply conservative President acting in accord with the nation's most important business interests—what we now call The Establishment—to protect business from the reform elements in the nation. Kolko maintains that Roosevelt's attempt to impose federal control upon business effectively eliminated the possibility of stronger measures being enacted by the individual states. Kolko further suggests that although Roosevelt and J. P. Morgan appeared to be adversaries throughout Roosevelt's presidency, on questions such as the need for some governmental control of business and the senselessness of unlimited and expensive competition, they were in basic agreement. In this selection Kolko argues that Roosevelt's presidential reform program was essentially conservative and that Roosevelt's reputation as a foe of big business interests is undeserved.

From Gabriel Kolko, *The Triumph of Conservatism* (New York: The Free Press, 1963), pp. 65–78 and 127–132. Reprinted by permission of The Macmillan Company. Copyright 1963 by The Free Press of Glencoe, a Division of The Macmillan Company.

A New President

During the first year of his presidency, Roosevelt moved as cautiously on the trust issue as McKinley would have. He inherited McKinley's Attorney General, Philander Knox—formerly attorney for Andrew Carnegie—and the equivocal Republican trust plank written by Mark Hanna. Moreover, the Republican Party was still dominated by Hanna. But, most important of all, Roosevelt had no firm convictions on the question of antitrust policy. His Message to the New York Legislature on the question in January, 1900, was in large part a verbatim transcription of a letter that had been sent him by Elihu Root —the lawyer of Thomas Fortune Ryan and other major capitalists— in December, 1899. He had never written on the question, his understanding of economics was conventional if not orthodox, and his expressions on larger questions of social and economic policy were decidedly conservative. As Governor of New York he had cooperated handsomely with George Perkins and the New York Life Insurance Company in quashing a bill passed by the Legislature limiting the amount of insurance which could be carried by any state-chartered company. Perkins, in return, was very active at the Republican national convention in winning the vice-presidential nomination for Roosevelt, a conscious step, as John Morton Blum rightly suggests, in advancing the political career of Roosevelt. His relationship to Mark Hanna was proper, if not cordial, and Hanna's differences with Roosevelt were those of conflicting personal ambitions and not of principle. Hanna was as pro-union as one could be without giving up a commitment to the open shop. He, like McKinley, favored moderate action—or statements—on the trust issue, and he defended the economic advantages of corporate concentration in much the same terms as Roosevelt later did. The relationship between business and government was essentially a pragmatic one. More fundamental questions did not have to be discussed simply because neither Hanna nor Roosevelt conceived of a governmental policy which challenged in a fundamental manner the existing social and economic relationships. Both men took that relationship for granted. Both accepted the desirability of a conservative trade union movement, responsible business, industrial conciliation, and government action to stop the "menace of today . . . the spread of a spirit of socialism" among workers. Both allied themselves with the pro-conservative union, pro-big business, welfare-oriented National Civic Federation.

Roosevelt's first Annual Message to Congress, on December 3, 1901, was carefully shaped to suit all tastes. Roosevelt discussed the matter with George Perkins, now a Morgan partner, at the beginning of October, and gave him a first draft for his comments and recommendations. Perkins regarded the draft as perfectly acceptable, and was particularly pleased by the section endorsing national rather than state regulation; but Roosevelt apparently mistook a few critical comments for opposition. He wrote to Douglas Robinson that he considered his older views on the topic to be "no longer sufficient." "I intend to be most conservative, but in the interests of the big corporations themselves and above all in the interest of the country I intend to pursue, cautiously but steadily, the course to which I have been publicly committed again and again. . . ." His old position in the New York Legislature, on one hand, was insufficient, but his insistence on carrying through "the course to which I have been publicly committed again and again" indicates Roosevelt was in reality most unsure of his course. To play it safe, however, he told Robinson he would "in strict secrecy let you show such parts of it as you think best to prominent men from whom we think we can get advantageous suggestions or who may state objections. . . ."

By the time Perkins, Robert Bacon, another Morgan partner, and assorted "prominent men" got through with the draft, virtually nothing in Roosevelt's Message warranted anxieties on their part. His statement was a defense, if not a eulogy, of big business. "The process [of industrial development] has aroused much antagonism, a great part of which is wholly without warrant. It is not true that as the rich have grown richer the poor have grown poorer. . . . The captains of industry who have driven the railway systems across this continent, who have built up our commerce, who have developed our manufactures, have on the whole done great good to our people." Success was based on ability, and foolish attacks on corporations would hinder our position in the world market. "It cannot too often be pointed out that to strike with ignorant violence at the interests of one set of men almost inevitably endangers the interests of all." With the welfare of the nation thus dependent on the security and stability of big business, Roosevelt then attacked the "reckless agitator" and made it clear that "The mechanism of modern business is so delicate that extreme care must be taken not to interfere with it in a spirit of rashness or ignorance." Occasional evils that did arise, such as overcapitalization, could be taken care of by publicity, and "Publicity is the only sure remedy which we can now evoke." And, as a final gesture of goodwill to business, Roosevelt advocated the supremacy of federal over state legislation as the solution to the anarchy of dozens of distinct state laws.

Such caution was indeed gratifying. But Roosevelt's next step was less pleasing, if not surprising. Philander Knox, certainly no radical before or after the Northern Securities Case, opened the case against the Northern Securities Company on behalf of the federal government. The details of the incident have been discussed in every standard history of the period. Suffice it to say here that the effort of the Harriman railroad interests to reach a formal accord with the Morgan-Hill interests to end internecine competition for the control of the Chicago, Burlington & Quincy Railroad via joint ownership resulted only in banning the formal device of the holding company. The actual ownership of the railroad by the two power blocs was not altered, nor did they have to give up their railroad holdings, which still faced competition for three-quarters of their traffic. Preparation of the case was begun secretly by Knox, and not even Elihu Root was consulted. Perhaps it is true that Roosevelt wanted to assert the power of the Presidency over Wall Street, or aggrandize his ego, but neither precedent nor the subsequent events justify such a view. The agitation for action against the company was intense in the Midwest, but this alone does not explain the event.

The Northern Securities Case was a politically popular act, and it has strongly colored subsequent historical interpretations of Roosevelt as a trustbuster. It did not change the railroad situation in the Northwest, the ownership of the railroads in that region, nor did it end cooperation among the Hill–Morgan and Harriman lines. Roosevelt never asked for a dissolution of the company, or a restoration of competition. Knox' motives can be evaluated quite explicitly, and Roosevelt's intentions in the matter can be judged largely on the basis of his subsequent actions. Knox certainly never intended to restore competition among the involved railroads, and his concept of alternatives never reached a sufficiently articulate condition to allow either him or Roosevelt to shape the course of events toward some significant change. "The final solution," Knox mused, "by which the good of combination will be preserved for the community and the evils be excluded, may combine a just measure of scope for the operation of both principles—competition, which is the healthful economic reminder of the law of the 'survival of the fittest,' and combination which is the economic expression of the social force of cooperation; and both these forces may therefore in this ultimate solution properly modify yet support each other, rather than destroy and exclude." Regulated combinations, he predicted, will "show even greater common benefits." At about the same time, Knox did not think there was anything incongruous in asking Henry Clay Frick, his former client and a major shareholder in Morgan's United States Steel, to invest large sums of money for him in Pittsburgh banks.

The Northern Securities Case caught Wall Street by surprise, less because it actually damaged concrete interests than because it seemed to threaten the autonomy of the business decision-making process. This is not to say that business did not desire government regulation in certain areas, but this was surely not one of them. The classic version of Morgan's response has it that J. P. Morgan, who allegedly regarded the President as little more than a businessman in politics, visited Washington on March 10, 1902, to discuss the threatened change in Washington–Wall Street relations with Roosevelt. The discussion, according to the initial source, included the following dialogue:

> "If we have done anything wrong," said Mr. Morgan, "send your man (meaning the Attorney General) to my man (naming one of his lawyers) and they can fix it up." "That can't be done," said the President. "We don't want to fix it up," added Mr. Knox, "we want to stop it." Then Mr. Morgan asked: "Are you going to attack my other interests, the Steel Trust and the others?" "Certainly not," replied the President, "unless we find out that in any case they have done something that we regard as wrong."

Certain aspects of the version are incorrect on their face value. Neither Roosevelt nor Knox ever intended "to stop it" if by that term it is meant to dissolve the basic structure of ownership or control in any industry. The significance of the discussion has never been fully appreciated. Morgan made an offer, and whether he consciously decided for it at the time or not, Roosevelt operationally accepted it. Indeed, the event was the most decisive in the subsequent history of Roosevelt's trust policy.

In June, 1902, Perkins approached Roosevelt, Knox, Root, and others about the government designating "some safe plan for us to adopt" in forming the International Mercantile Marine Company. Knox refused to comment on the scheme Perkins presented, but it is evident that the House of Morgan was quite serious about obtaining a government dispensation for its undertakings—especially since, in this case, a subsidy from Congress for the new shipping company was also desired. Their belief that such a détente might be arranged was undoubtedly stimulated by Roosevelt's speeches. "The line of demarcation we draw must always be on conduct, not on wealth; our objection to any given corporation must be, not that it is big, but that it behaves badly." At the same time, Roosevelt turned to Perkins for aid in passing his first important legislation for federal regulation of industry.

Agitation for a Department of Commerce had been carried on by business organizations throughout the 1890's. The idea was not particularly controversial and was especially welcomed by advocates of expanded foreign trade; only lethargy and a desire to reduce expenditures prevented earlier action. Big business sentiment for comprehensive federal regulation eliminating troublesome state regulation also stimulated interest in a federal agency that might lead to this end. Federal incorporation seemed to hold out the possibility of solving these problems, and "Affording the protection of the national government against conflicting state legislation and local political enactments, and—what is equally important—enforcing well-considered regulations and wholesome restrictions incidental to national institutions . . ."—as the important corporation lawyer, James B. Dill, phrased it. Roosevelt's Second Message to Congress in December, 1902, couched in soothing, conservative terms, asked Congress to create a Department of Commerce. "A fundamental base of civilization is the inviolability of property." State regulation could not adequately prevent the misuse of corporate power that was possible. In calling for national regulation, Roosevelt insistently repeated that "Our aim is not to do away with corporations; on the contrary, these big aggregations are an inevitable development of modern industrialism, and the effort to destroy them would be futile unless accomplished in ways that would work the utmost mischief to the entire body politic." Making it clear where his loyalties lay, Roosevelt developed his commitment even further by suggesting, in a manner similar to France's comment on the rich man and poor man in a democracy having the equal right to sleep under the bridge at night, that he was not at all interested in a redistribution of wealth or power. "We are neither for the rich man as such nor for the poor man as such; we are for the upright man, rich or poor." The problems incident to an industrial society, therefore, could be solved by a higher personal morality, and nothing was more conducive to personal morality than publicity.

To aid him in his efforts for regulation, Roosevelt turned to the conservative Republican and business elements. Bring pressure to bear on Speaker David B. Henderson to secure passage of the Department of Commerce Bill, he wrote Perkins in late December, 1902, and have Marshall Field see that Rep. James R. Mann, chairman of the Interstate and Foreign Commerce Committee, brings in "a thoroughly sensible report" on the topic.

Perkins assured Roosevelt that he wanted the bill passed, and that the wheels were already moving. His legislative agent in Washington, William C. Beer, kept him fully informed of the progress of their joint efforts. At the same time, Perkins had Senator Joseph B. Foraker of Ohio ask Roosevelt about the possibility of additional trust prosecutions, and the Senator could confidently report that "nothing will be done *at present,* and I am confident nothing will be done hereafter."

A bill to create a Department of Commerce and Labor passed the Senate in January, 1902. It made no progress getting through the House Committee on Interstate and Foreign Commerce until January, 1903, shortly after Perkins took up the task. Amended to the House Bill, however, was a provision for a Bureau of Corporations—the Administration's potential agency for publicity on corporate affairs. The Administration directed its efforts in January, 1903, toward the passage of the Nelson amendment and toward the defeat of the

Littlefield resolution. The Nelson amendment—written by Knox at Roosevelt's request—would allow the President to withhold information gathered by the Bureau of Corporations, thereby using publicity as his major tool for policing corporations, and would give the bureau the right to obtain whatever testimony or documents it deemed necessary. Roosevelt, in effect, could decide at his own discretion which corporations to attack through publicity. The Littlefield resolution, which passed the House, would have required all corporations engaged in interstate commerce to file annual financial reports with the Interstate Commerce Commission. Its major provision barred from interstate commerce any corporation which used discriminatory rates or sought to destroy competition. Roosevelt and Knox made their opposition to the measure known in early January: they preferred publicity to destruction, and the Littlefield Bill was stopped in the Senate. Roosevelt gave all of his support to the passage of the Nelson amendment to the Department of Commerce Bill.

Passage of the bill was inevitable, but was given a sudden burst of support by a *faux pas* committed by John D. Rockefeller, Jr. On February 6, Rockefeller wired Senators Allison, Lodge, Hale, and Teller that Standard opposed the Bureau of Corporations Bill. Roosevelt seized upon the opportunity and called in the press, transforming Rockefeller, Jr. into Rockefeller, Sr., and exaggerating the number of Senators that had received the telegram—but his story was essentially correct. This gave the measure an aura of radicalism to alienated Congressmen irritated by Roosevelt's conservative opposition to the Littlefield resolution, and it undoubtedly made a few indifferent Congressmen vote for the bill. On February 10, the House passed the bill 252 to 10, and the next day the Senate casually approved the bill without debate or a roll call. Roosevelt signed his bill on February 14, and later sent one of the pens he used to George Perkins, telling him "Your interest in the legislation was strongly indicated at different times during the year or more of active discussion. . . ."

The Bureau of Corporations Bill passed with conservative support and was motivated by conservative intentions. Perkins had actively campaigned for it, and the Department of Commerce aspect of the bill was welcomed by all businessmen. "You know that I have the highest hopes for the new Department, and sincerely believe that it will be of very great practical use to our Government and our vast business interests," Perkins wrote Roosevelt in July, 1903. Despite Standard Oil efforts to dissuade him, Senator Nelson Aldrich worked with Roosevelt in the passage of the bill, and Roosevelt relied on him at various times. Roosevelt, after all, had destroyed the radical Littlefield proposal, and nothing in his presidency justified serious apprehension as to what he might do with the new bureau. William Howard Taft, ironically, chided Roosevelt about his reliance on the conservatives in Congress, and the President's rationale for his cooperation with them was based not only on political opportunism but also on the inherent desirability of the alliance. "My experience for the last year and a half . . . has made me feel respect and regard for Aldrich as one of that group of Senators, including Allison, Hanna, Spooner, Platt . . . Lodge and one or two others, who, together with men like the next Speaker of the House, Joe Cannon, are the most powerful factors in Congress." He might differ with them on specific questions, but they were "not only essential to work with, but desirable to work with . . . and it was far more satisfactory to work with them than to try to work with the radical 'reformers,' like Littlefield."

The Executive and Business

Roosevelt's cooperation with Aldrich continued as a matter of course, and the President sought out the elder statesman's advice on crucial issues. "I would like to read over to you a couple of my speeches in which I shall touch on the trusts and the tariff. . . . I want to be sure to get what I say on these two subjects along lines upon which all of us can agree," he wrote to Aldrich in March, 1903. At the same time, George M. Cortelyou, the first Secretary of Commerce, assured George Perkins "We are making good progress in the organization of the Department [of Commerce] on careful, conservative lines." The assurance was based on fact. In February, immediately after the passage of the law, Roosevelt asked James R. Garfield to assume the post of Commissioner of Corporations and direct the new bureau. Garfield's assets, so far as Roosevelt was concerned, were many, not the least of them being his tennis ability, which qualified him for Roosevelt's "tennis cabinet." Son of President Garfield, civil service reformer, active in Ohio Republican politics, Garfield also had powerful friends among businessmen. Francis Lynde Stetson, a fellow alumnus of Williams College who often saw Garfield at old school functions, was consulted and gave the approval of the House of Morgan. The Cabinet approved of the appointment, and although Hanna did not care for Garfield, a meeting between the two and a profession of conservative intent by Garfield won the political leader over. Moreover, Garfield was friendly with important Standard Oil lawyers.

In August, Roosevelt became concerned that the overcapitalization of many recent corporate promotions, especially by Morgan, was the cause of the recent stock market panic. But throughout the year Roosevelt retained the support of Republican conservatives, such as Platt, who advised his Wall Street friends to give direction to the essentially conservative Roosevelt and try to control him. Roosevelt's Third Annual Message to Congress on December 7, 1903, confirmed Platt's estimate of the President: Roosevelt stressed that the organization of the Department of Commerce and the Bureau of Corporations "proceeded on sane and conservative lines." Legitimate business and labor had nothing to fear from publicity, and the new organizations would not only lead to conciliation between capital and labor but to a better position in foreign trade as well. "We recognize that this is an era of federation and combination, in which great capitalistic corporations and labor unions have become factors of tremendous importance in all industrial centers."

The Bureau of Corporations' major activity during its first year of existence was to define its own legal functions in corporate regulation and those of the national government as well. The issue of the federal regulation of insurance, and whether it could be considered a form of commerce, was, as we shall see, very popular among insurance men—and a number of studies on the problem were prepared by the bureau's legal staff. So far as federal incorporation was concerned, bureau experts concluded, Congress had the power to regulate corporations. Surely, it seemed, the Bureau of Corporations gave big business little to fear and at least something to hope for.

Not a few businessmen remained unhappy with the President, however. Roosevelt retained the support of such conservative Republicans as Senator Joseph B. Foraker of Ohio, Aldrich, and Elihu Root, but the Supreme Court decision in 1904 confirming the Northern Securities prosecution, and the creation of a distinct appropriation—however minute—within the Justice Department for antitrust work, raised some apprehension. "I say to you that he has been . . . the greatest conservative force for the protection of property and our institutions in the city of Washington," Elihu Root warned his peers at the Union Club of New York in February, 1904. "Never forget that the men who labor cast the votes, set up and pull down governments. . . ." The presence of men such as Root, Cortelyou, Paul Morton, Taft, Knox and many other former members of the business and social elite, as well as most of McKinley's major appointees, still testified to the conservative nature of the Administration. Moreover, Roosevelt filed only three antitrust suits in 1902, two in 1903, and one in 1904. There was perhaps a little bluster now and again, but virtually no bite, and big business knew it.

Business had many reasons for optimism as far as the Bureau of Corporations was concerned. And in December, 1902, Roosevelt invited Judge Elbert H. Gary to the White House. The President had never met the chairman of United States Steel, but the two men immediately took a liking to each other, and saw each other and communicated frequently over the next seven years. This mutual confidence was to be of vast importance.

In May, 1904, the Interstate Commerce Commission found the Morgan-controlled International Harvester Company guilty of obtaining rebates from an Illinois railroad which it owned. Earlier in the year Cyrus McCormick had told Commissioner Garfield that so far as the Bureau of Corporations' program was concerned, ". . . International Harvester was in entire sympathy with some program of this sort." Instead of prosecuting it, Attorney General William H. Moody and Garfield agreed to an International Harvester proposal that if the company would in the future conform to the law after being told when and where it was violating it, the right of prosecution would be dropped; no formal means of fulfilling the agreement appears to have been arranged. That George Perkins had organized the company, and was the major Morgan representative in it, was probably of influence in the bureau's having so lenient an attitude. At about the same time, Garfield discussed his plans for the bureau with Virgil P. Kline, counsel for Standard Oil and a friend, and Kline relayed the information to H. H. Rogers. The bureau wanted information, and Garfield intimated it would not be used for purposes of prosecution. In June, 1904, according to Garfield, Kline told him "the

Standard Oil Company would cooperate with the Bureau and would give me the information that I desire . . ." for a bureau study. They agreed that "we would confer with the representatives of the company" on all important matters related to the study and bureau plans.

Garfield was rapidly formulating a course of action for the Bureau of Corporations that was to operationally determine the nature of Roosevelt's trust policies. In March, 1904, in response to pressure from livestock growers, the House passed a resolution calling for a bureau investigation of beef prices and profits. Garfield did not want the job, but was forced to proceed nevertheless. In April and in subsequent months, working through Charles G. Dawes of the Central Trust Company of Chicago, Garfield met with the major Chicago packers and assured them any information he obtained would remain confidential and that he had no intention of harming their interests. Even before a formal policy on the function of the Bureau of Corporations had been formulated, Garfield had moved to make the organization a shield behind which business might seek protection. Informal détentes and understandings were regarded sympathetically, even if the law was circumvented, and nothing would be done to harm business interests.

The pending election did a great deal, of course, to mitigate any radical action Roosevelt might have contemplated. In September and October, 1904, Garfield and Roosevelt came to an understanding as to the nature and function of the bureau. Garfield decided that "The function of the Bureau of Corporations is not to enforce the antitrust laws," or even to gather information indicating the need for their enforcement. Roosevelt was less clear as to whether its purpose was to gather information to enforce existing laws or to show what additional legislation might be necessary, but Garfield's position was to prevail. Information gathered by the bureau would be released only at the discretion of the President—as provided by the law—and even though the beef information gathered by the bureau was not given to the U.S. District Attorney of northern Illinois, then considering legal measures, the names of the bureau's informants were passed along. The bureau was charged with investigating for purposes of possible legislation, not enforcing existing laws, Garfield maintained, and its information could not be used by other departments for purposes of prosecution. ". . . the policy of obtaining hearty

cooperation rather than arousing antagonism of business and industrial interests has been followed," he concluded.

Garfield had, in fact, been most cooperative with business. And
rather than recommending legislation, the bureau effectively served,
with its time-consuming procedures, as a block to legislation. "The
danger of remedial legislation," Garfield wrote, "is that in its efforts
to strike down the abnormal, the unusual and the evil, it likewise
strike[s] down the normal, the usual and the good, hence extreme
remedial legislation results in disaster." Garfield was giving the bureau a safe, conservative direction. Roosevelt was safe too, and so
was the Republican platform he ran on in 1904. "Combinations of
capital and of labor are the results of the economic movement of
the age, but neither must be permitted to infringe upon the rights
and interests of the people. Such combinations, when lawfully
formed for lawful purposes, are alike entitled to the protection of
the laws, but both are subject to the laws and neither can be permitted to break them." Thus having equated the power of the corporation with the power of a puny craft union movement, the
Republicans resigned themselves to the movement of the age. Despite Roosevelt's insistence that the Party return a large donation
from Standard Oil, the Roosevelt campaign received large sums of
money from Perkins, E. H. Harriman, and businessmen convinced
by Root—who was shaping many of Roosevelt's campaign speeches
—and others in the Administration that the President was doing his
best for business.

It is possible, of course, that the commonly held conception of
Roosevelt as the anticorporate radical biding his time until he was
President by virtue of a ballot box, not an anarchist's bullets, is valid.
But certainly nothing the President did or said in the months immediately following his victory in 1904 justifies such an interpretation.
Quite the contrary, the remainder of Roosevelt's presidency was
essentially a continuation of his first three years, adjusted for tan-
gential personal qualities and idiosyncrasies. Perhaps Roosevelt
may have conceived of himself as an impartial, objective mediator
between contending economic interests, seeking to mitigate class
conflicts. "It would be a dreadful calamity," he wrote Philander Knox
in November, "if we saw this country divided into two parties, one
containing the bulk of the property owners and conservative people,

the other the bulk of the wageworkers and the less prosperous people generally." Roosevelt persistently returned to this theme—reform
to him was a means of preventing radical social change. And inevitably, as if by reflex, he identified himself with conservatism and a
benevolent paternalism. "The friends of property, of order, of law,
must never show weakness in the face of violence or wrong or injustice; but on the other hand . . . it is peculiarly incumbent upon the
man with whom things have prospered to be in a certain sense the
keeper of his brother with whom life has gone hard." It never oc-
curred to Roosevelt, who dwelt on this theme again in his Message
to Congress on December 6, that the existing distribution of power
was based on something more than talent and personal skill. "Great
corporations are necessary, and only men of great and singular mental power can manage such corporations successfully, and such men
must have great rewards." This did not justify unabashed exploitation, because Roosevelt nominally placed "good sense, courage, and
kindliness" on a higher scale of priorities. But translated into specific terms, this always resulted in a defense of business interests, and
a call for mutual charity between the unequal—"More important than
any legislation is the gradual growth of a feeling of responsibility
and forbearance among capitalists and wageworkers alike."

Business was indeed gratified by the President's and Garfield's
conservatism. The bureau's policy, Roosevelt announced in the only
aspect of his 1904 Message bearing on industrial corporations, was
"one of open inquiry into, and not attack upon, business, [and] the
Bureau has been able to gain not only the confidence, but, better
still, the cooperation of men engaged in legitimate business." Garfield's first report for the bureau, in December, 1904, was similarly
reassuring.

*In brief, the policy of the Bureau in the accomplishment of the purposes
of its creation is to cooperate with, not antagonize, the business world;
the immediate object of its inquiries is the suggestion of constructive
legislation, not the institution of criminal prosecutions. It purposes,
through exhaustive investigations of law and fact, to secure conservative
action, and to avoid ill-considered attack upon corporations charged with
unfair or dishonest practices. Legitimate business—law-respecting persons and corporations—have nothing to fear from the proposed exercise
of this great governmental power of inquiry.*

Moreover, Garfield came out for federal licensing of corporations, and this was especially welcomed by many big businessmen. "After the first year," Garfield reported later, "the business interests of the country appreciated that the Bureau was not to be used as an instrument of improper inquisition. . . ." With the exception of Francis Lynde Stetson, who did not like the idea of federal incorporation and represented only himself, spokesmen of business were delighted with Garfield's report and few were apprehensive about what Roosevelt might do next. Even Stetson was pleased with the other work of the bureau. Seth Low, chairman of the National Civic Federation and an important influence in Roosevelt's trust policies, approved heartily. Perkins called Garfield up and congratulated him, and Garfield responded by welcoming any suggestions he or his business friends might have. Business communications were overwhelmingly in favor of Garfield's report and proposal. John D. Rockefeller, Sr., praised Garfield's license plan, according to *Harper's Weekly*, because "the Federal government would scarcely issue its license to a corporation without at the same time guaranteeing to its beneficiaries an adequate degree of protection."

The *Wall Street Journal* editorialized on December 28, 1904:

> *Nothing is more noteworthy than the fact that President Roosevelt's recommendation in favor of government regulation of railroad rates and Commissioner Garfield's recommendation in favor of federal control of interstate companies have met with so much favor among managers of railroad and industrial companies. It is not meant by this that much opposition has not developed, for it has, but it might have been expected that the financial interests in control of the railroads and the industrial corporations would be unanimous in antagonism to these measures, which would, if carried into effect, deprive them of so much of their present power.*
>
> *The fact is that many of the railroad men and corporation managers are known to be in favor of these measures, and this is of vast significance. In the end it is probable that all of the corporations will find that a reasonable system of federal regulation is to their interest. It is not meant by this that the financial interests who are in favor of the administrative measures, approve of them exactly in the shape in which they have been presented by the President and Commissioner Garfield, but with the principle of the thing they are disposed to agree.*
>
> *. . . Now as between governmental regulation by forty-five states and governmental regulation by the central authority of the federal govern-*

ment, there can be but one choice. . . . The choice must be that of a federal regulation, for that will be uniform over the whole country and of a higher and more equitable standard. . . .

The Rule of Reason

One can evaluate Roosevelt's relationship to big business both operationally and theoretically. Operationally there is the reality of détentes with the Morgan companies, and the President's refusal to take steps against them. At the same time there is the fact that the antitrust activity of Roosevelt's Administration was purely minimal, and substantially less, in terms of the number of cases initiated, than under Taft or Warren G. Harding.

Even without discounting Roosevelt's more exuberant political rhetoric, there was a remarkable correspondence between these operational realities and his theories. Although his views on the relationship of the corporation to society and politics developed somewhat through experience, the core of his ideas remained remarkably constant. He usually discussed the corporation in the context of an attack on "sinister demagogs and foolish visionaries" who "seek to excite a violent class hatred against all men of wealth." The corporation that created injustice, and the critic of injustice who did not accept the basic premises of the corporate economy, were invariably equated, and the injustices that Roosevelt attacked were not the structural evils inherent in an exploitive economy but those evils associated with a few exceptional corporations. "Under no circumstances would we countenance attacks upon law-abiding property," he declared in January, 1908, "or do ought but condemn those who hold up rich men as being evil men because of their riches. On the contrary, our whole effort is to insist upon conduct, and neither wealth nor property nor any other class distinction, as being the proper standard by which to judge the actions of men." Conduct, to Roosevelt, was a personal and not an institutional question, and in reality often was equated with the manners and class sensibilities upon which Roosevelt had been raised. "Sweeping attacks upon all property, upon all men of means, without regard to whether they do well or ill, would sound the death-knell of the Republic," he never tired of reiterating.

"In the modern industrial world combinations are absolutely necessary," Roosevelt concluded, and not merely among businessmen but among workers and farmers as well. Roosevelt resigned himself to the contemporary belief in the inevitability of trusts. "It is mischievous and unwholesome," he repeated again and again in different ways, "to keep upon the statute books unmodified, a law, like the anti-trust law, which, while in practice only partially effective against vicious combinations, has nevertheless in theory been construed so as sweepingly to prohibit every combination for the transaction of modern business." The law should not be repealed, he declared in December, 1907, but "it should be so amended as to forbid only the kind of combination which does harm to the general public." Combinations were "reasonable or unreasonable," and the way to determine which should be allowed was to grant supervisory power to the federal government. Antitrust suits as a means of enforcing the law, Roosevelt declared, were "irksome" and prolonged affairs. Instead, the government should have the right to approve "reasonable agreements" between corporations, provided they were submitted for approval to an "appropriate" body. National incorporation of combinations, with heavy emphasis of the regular publication of key data and publicity, would allow the government to regulate the corporate structure to protect both shareholders and the public. Barring this, federal licensing for the same ends might be tried. And only the national government was capable of effective regulation of this magnitude. Regulation, not repression, was the theme.

Roosevelt's interpretation of the trust problem, his association of the evils of concentration with the personality of individuals, and his separation of "good" from "bad" combinations as a means of accepting the major premises of the corporate economy, were all part of the dominant thought of the day. His basic ideas, which were virtually identical to the attitude on the "trust problem" taken by the big business supporters of the National Civic Federation, were eminently acceptable to the corporate elite. The idea of federal incorporation or licensing was attractive as a shield against state regulation, and rather than frightening big business, as most historians believe they did, Roosevelt's statements encouraged them. Indeed, even his passing reference in his 1906 Message to Congress to the theoretical desirability of an income tax law was hardly radical. Andrew Carnegie was also attacking the unequal distribution of wealth as "one of the crying evils of our day," and the fact that Roosevelt took no concrete steps on the matter, and linked it with a Constitutional amendment, meant his rhetoric was not frightening even to reactionaries.

Early in 1908, George W. Perkins, the functional architect of the détente system and political capitalism during Roosevelt's presidency, attempted to articulate a systematic view on the relationship of the giant corporation to national government. The modern corporation, to Perkins, was the "working of natural causes of evolution." It must welcome federal supervision, administered by practical businessmen, that "should say to stockholders and the public from time to time that the management's reports and methods of business are correct." With federal regulation, which would free business from the many states, industrial cooperation could replace competition. In a defense of Roosevelt against unwarranted attacks from the business community—a community that was not obtaining the same benefits of business-government cooperation as Morgan firms —Perkins also suggested that Roosevelt shared his interpretation of the necessity of sympathetic regulation. "It is needless to say that I am in substantial agreement with most of the propositions that it contains," Roosevelt wrote his admirer upon receiving a copy of the speech.

With the exception of Bonaparte, virtually all of Roosevelt's important advisers accepted his interpretation of the trust issue. Roosevelt ignored Bonaparte's objection that the terms "reasonable" and "unreasonable" were too indefinite for legal purposes and were subject to arbitrary interpretation. He did not feel that the antitrust law should be sweepingly applied, which it never was, but he suggested that Roosevelt's past distinctions between good and bad trusts had caused "those interested in certain trusts to claim immunity on the ground of their virtuous and benevolent purposes." The détente system, Bonaparte sensed, was the logical conclusion of Roosevelt's philosophy. He was correct, but his influence was not sufficient to override it. Bonaparte, like his peers, was never concerned with the size of the corporate unit, but only with whether it violated the law. The difference was that the literal-minded Bonaparte thought an inflexible law was desirable, and Roosevelt did not. Roosevelt sharply distinguished between good and bad corporations, and if the contemporary public was largely unaware of the subtle differences, at least Roosevelt and many big businessmen knew precisely what was happening. Roosevelt was consciously using government regulation to save the capitalist system, perhaps even from itself, for the greatest friend of socialism was the unscrupulous businessman who did not recognize that moderate regulation could save him from a more drastic fate in the hands of the masses. ". . . I think the worst thing that could be done," he wrote Henry Lee Higginson concerning the railroads, "would be an announcement that for two or three years the Federal Government would keep its hands off of them. It would result in a tidal wave of violent State action against them thruout three-fourths of this country." "The reactionary or ultraconservative apologists for the misuse of wealth assail the effort to secure such control as a step toward socialism. As a matter of fact it is these reactionaries and ultraconservatives who are themselves most potent in increasing socialistic feeling." ". . . we are acting in the defense of property," he reminded Lodge.

Roosevelt was not alone in reiterating his conservative intent and function. Elihu Root as Secretary of State and L. M. Shaw as Secretary of the Treasury were two of the bitterest opponents of popular government. Oscar S. Straus, his Secretary of Commerce from December, 1906 on, was formerly president of the New York Board of Trade and Transportation, and was close to the National Civic Federation; he allowed Herbert Knox Smith to run the Bureau of Corporations with a free hand. More interested in immigration problems than corporations, Straus was personally close to various New York banking interests.

Key businessmen knew that Roosevelt relied heavily on Nelson Aldrich, especially for banking and financial advice, and that major machine politicians, such as Boies Penrose, could publicly proclaim their alliance with Roosevelt without a denial from the President. But their most important connection remained the Bureau of Corporations and its commissioners, first Garfield and then Herbert Knox Smith. Garfield went to great extremes during the formation of the bureau to assure that "the business interests of the country appreciated that the Bureau was not to be used as an instrument of improper inquisition nor, as some of the extremists feared, blackmail." Upon leaving the bureau he wrote Straus that "the work of the Bureau has shown the absurdity of the antitrust act," and the need for federal supervision. Smith took virtually the same position as Garfield and Roosevelt.

Important businessmen were fully aware and appreciative of the policies of Roosevelt and his chief aides, and hardly succumbed to the irritated clamor of the conservative press that criticized the President on the basis of deduction from its abstract theories rather than on an evaluation of his concrete actions. Roosevelt's special conflict with Harriman, which initially had nothing to do with the tycoon's conduct as a railroad operator, was caused by a conflicting interpretation of the basis on which Harriman had donated funds to the 1904 campaign. Until late 1905 their relationship was perfectly amiable, and even after the breach in their relationship Roosevelt never took antitrust action against any of the Harriman roads, despite the fact that Harriman and Standard Oil became the criteria for "bad" and "unreasonable" trusts. And big businessmen such as Perkins, Gary, and the leadership of the National Civic Federation, which included among its ranks Seth Low, August Belmont, Andrew Carnegie, and John Hays Hammond, knew better than most of their contemporaries that the Roosevelt Administration was eminently acceptable ideologically and politically.

The key to their appreciation of Roosevelt was his antitrust policies. During October, 1907, the National Civic Federation held a large trust conference in Chicago to develop its viewpoint on the inevitability and desirability of the large corporation. "There is, in my opinion, more danger to be feared from the ordinary tendencies of the various States than from the present National Administration or any future National Administration," Isaac N. Seligman told the gathering. Charles G. Dawes, Nicholas Murray Butler, Robert Mather, Herbert Knox Smith, and numerous lawyers, businessmen, and public figures rose to expound the basic principles of Roosevelt's economic philosophy. At the conclusion of the convention, and virtually unanimously, the gathering called for legislation to permit "Business and industrial agreements or combinations whose objects are in the public interest . . . ," the exclusion of unions and farmers' organizations from the jurisdiction of the Sherman Act, federal incorporation laws, and the expansion of the publicity functions of various federal agencies regulating business. They also called for a public commission to recommend comprehensive trust legislation.

IV ROOSEVELT AND THE PROGRESSIVE PARTY

Donald Richberg

WE THOUGHT IT WAS ARMAGEDDON

Donald Richberg was a young lawyer who suddenly found himself a central figure in Roosevelt's new Progressive Party in 1912. His memoir of the excitement, significance, and magic of the Bull Moose crusade is one of the best descriptions of the appeal of Roosevelt's third party.

The streets were packed with people shouting: "We want Teddy." It was June, 1912. He stood up in his automobile at the door of the hotel and spoke briefly. I remember only the words, "Thou shalt not steal," and the eastern accent that so surprised me. This "rough-rider" spoke like the men I had heard in Harvard Yard, many years before. The first glimpse of Roosevelt confirmed the impression I had when I described him in my book of the previous year as "the Apostle of the Obvious." Filling the same role on the next Monday evening, he spoke in the Auditorium and finished with, "We stand at Armageddon and we battle for the Lord."

"It's too bad he can't leave the Bible and the Lord out of this row," I complained to a sympathetic newspaper man. But a few weeks later we shook the steel beams of the Coliseum with *Onward Christian Soldiers* and a politics-hardened reporter telegraphed his New York editor: "I can't make fun of this convention. This is a religion."

The progressive movement of 1912 was religious; a revolt of youth against age, of idealism against materialism. My generation was spoiling for a fight with the ancient enemies of progress—the self-satisfied. It was sick and tired of pot-bellied politicians; tired of bankers and business men preaching a one-day-in-seven version of the Golden Rule. It wanted to get religion, but not in churches patronized by thieves. So when T. R. located Armageddon and the band played marching hymns, we put on shining armor and went out to "battle for the Lord." It is altogether possible that the oncoming generation may do the same.

The Progressive Party did not spring full armed from the brain of Roosevelt. La Follette had been battling for twenty years before he

From *Survey*, Vol. LXI (March 1929), pp. 723–724.

was elected governor of Wisconsin in 1900; and it was his campaign for the Republican nomination in 1911 and 1912 that demonstrated the political power of the rising demand for "social justice." Bryan's leadership in the Democratic Party since 1896 had been based on the same appeal. Wilson was nominated in 1912 as the logical successor to this leadership. Prosperity was not enough. "If on this new continent we merely build another country of great but unjustly divided material prosperity, we shall have done nothing," said Roosevelt at Carnegie Hall in March, 1912.

Yet Wilson had expressed the pious hope that something could be done to "knock Bryan into a cocked hat"; and I have a personal letter from Roosevelt written in 1917, describing Senator La Follette as "one of the very few men who is distinctly worse than President Wilson." It appears that the outstanding leaders in the progressive movement disagreed rather vigorously regarding at least the methods of reaching the goal—if not the goal itself.

Now it happens that I worked intimately, for years, with Roosevelt and La Follette, that I had a long acquaintance and many associations with Bryan, and various close contacts with President Wilson's administration, as will appear hereafter. Upon this unprejudiced basis for appraising the public services of all these men, I know they were all truly "progressive"—in that their common goal was to lift up the level of the average well-being. Unfortunately they were so different in temperament, in personal habits and interests, which inevitably shape conduct, that not one could effectively cooperate with, or appreciate, the other. Yet, in his autobiography, La Follette wrote: "Roosevelt is the keenest and ablest living interpreter of what I would call the superficial sentiment of a given time and he is spontaneous in his response to it." In cruder, but quite forceful language, Medill McCormick, in a conference over platform-writing, once said: "Fellows, we must remember that T.R. is great because he understands the psychology of the mutt."

With these witnesses, fortified by my own experience, I have concluded that "Roosevelt progressivism" expressed more accurately the mass sentiment of my generation than the vague generalizations of the evangelic Bryan, the close reasoning of the uncompromising La Follette, or the erudite radicalism of Wilson. This "Roosevelt progressivism" did not question the existing order. It proposed changes in law, largely for the purpose of compelling or inducing men to be "good" instead of "bad." Public officials who behaved badly would be rejected, or their evil deeds would be annulled by popular vote. Employers would be directed to treat their employes well. Big business would be encouraged, if "good," and punished if "bad." The wicked strong people would be controlled and the good weak people would be protected.

This political program for bringing about "social justice" had several implications: 1. That there was a clear line between what was right and wrong. 2. That the People would vote right, if they had the chance. 3. That if public officials were responsive to public opinion, they would know what was right and would do it. Since the terrible lessons of the World War, it has become somewhat evident: 1. That what is right or wrong is frequently a question for scientific, rather than popular, opinion. 2. That the People can't vote right unless they have the capacity for right judgment. 3. That public officials, responsive to public opinion, may follow either propaganda or prejudice and neither know what is right, nor how to do it.

But the "Roosevelt progressivism" was based on what the Colonel well called a "confession of faith." It had a creed. You accepted it and joined the church. And so the Progressive National Convention was a great revival meeting. Prosperity was the natural ideal—not for the few, as Roosevelt pointed out, but for the many. Government should lift the poverty-stricken to the happy level of the well-to-do. In this glorious hour of political intoxication, the prophet Beveridge cried: "Pass Prosperity Around"; and at once a banner, already painted with the newborn slogan, fell from the ceiling. If not a miracle, this was at least a miraculous conception. We wept and we cheered and we sang, "His truth is marching on."

Medill McCormick wrinkled more deeply his youthful, furrowed brow and said: "Think of me and Jane Addams on the same platform!" But there also stood George W. Perkins and Judge Ben B. Lindsey and Bill Flinn of Pittsburgh and Raymond Robins of Chicago. There was room on that platform for any one who had seen Peter Pan and believed in fairies.

Amos Pinchot

ROOSEVELT AND THE DECLINE OF THE PROGRESSIVE PARTY

The Pinchot brothers, Amos and Gifford, were deeply involved with Theodore Roosevelt and the progressive movement. Gifford, the better known of the brothers, served as Roosevelt's Chief Forester and major adviser on conservation. Amos, on the other hand, became involved with Roosevelt's fortunes after his presidency; at that time Amos became a central figure in the new Progressive Party. In the late 1920's and early 1930's, Amos Pinchot decided to write the history of the Progressive Party. The manuscript languished unpublished in the Library of Congress until Helene Maxwell Hooker edited it for publication in 1958. The passages reprinted here contain some of the most incisive criticism ever written of Roosevelt and his Progressive Party. Unlike Donald Richberg, Amos Pinchot never felt the magic of Roosevelt's presence. This is the memoir of an insider who finds little to praise politically or morally in the Bull Moose movement.

As the 1912 presidential election drew near, the Morgan interests (and by this I mean especially the Steel Corporation, the largest and most successful industrial merger that has ever been launched) found themselves, politically speaking, in an extremely unsatisfactory position. Like other industro-financial powers of the kind, the Steel Corporation had been consistently Republican, and had helped Roosevelt in the defeat of Parker, coming to his rescue in the fall of 1904, when consternation gripped the Republican machine at the prospect of Parker's carrying the state of New York. It had entrenched itself strongly in the Roosevelt cabinet, shaped Roosevelt's economic thinking and the pro-trust policy of the industrial sections of his messages to Congress. It had spread, through the mouth of the President himself, Morgan's own pet distinction between good and bad trusts, which is still erroneously attributed to Roosevelt instead of Morgan. Through Gary and Perkins, it had made Roosevelt a sincere believer in the soundness of the giant merger system, and gained from him extravagant praise of the captains of industry and

Reprinted by permission of New York University Press from *History of the Progressive Party, 1912–1916*, by Amos R. E. Pinchot, edited and with a biographical introduction by Helene Maxwell Hooker. Copyright © 1958 by New York University Press, Inc., pp. 93–96, 229–231.

finance who were engineering these mergers. It had softened the President's heart to such an extent that he publicly defended the lavish salaries which these men were voting to themselves through docile boards of directors. It had wheedled Roosevelt into giving his indirect and innocent sanction to monopoly and various practices which we now regard as unsound and antisocial, but which were then on trial under the leadership of the Steel Corporation and the International Harvester Company, also a Morgan promotion. And, what was perhaps equally important, it had prevented the publication of the findings of the investigation of the Steel Corporation by Mr. H. K. Smith; and finally, had consolidated Morgan's monopoly power by getting the President's permission to buy its potential competitor, the Tennessee Coal and Iron Company, paying less than fifty million dollars in bonds for a concern whose mineral deposits alone were worth just under a billion, according to John Moody.

Most of these remarkable moves were made, unknown to the public, through the quiet and tactful intervention of the Gary-Perkins-Garfield group and the Morgan contingent in Roosevelt's entourage. But now, with the Republican party under Taft out of hand and plunged in economic heresy, the Morgan interests saw that they could look with almost as little satisfaction to the possibility of a Democratic administration in 1912. The surge of Northern capital toward the South had not yet taken place, and below Mason's and Dixon's line the agricultural interests were still rampantly anti-Wall Street. Both branches of Congress swarmed with Southern Democrats who would gladly play to their farm-bred constituents by abetting a steel or harvester trust prosecution. Brandeis and Augustus Stanley, chairman of the committee that had investigated the Steel Corporation in 1911 and 1912, were the two men who had dug more pitfalls in the path of the Steel Corporation's glorious advance than anyone else. Both were Southerners; both, as it happened, Kentuckians, and men of unusual intellectual force. Again, from the Steel Trust's point of view, democracy in the midwest section of the country held as little hope as in the South. It still smelled of populism and free silver; Bryan was again repeating his famous dictum to the effect that, if the government did not take over the railroads, the railroads would assuredly take over the government. And government ownership of the Morgan ore hauling roads would mean the end of the transportation differential that, as we have seen, upheld the trust's monopoly power and price-fixing power, and consequently the trust's vast profits which, according to Farquhar McRae, the statistician, amounted to 40 per cent of the cost of production.

In the East, a Democratic governor, New Jersey's rising star in the political firmament, was being groomed for the presidency under the tutelage of a clear-thinking, immensely able young lawyer, George L. Record, who knew both business and politics from the inside as well as any man of his time. Record was especially familiar with the technique of the Morgan steel merger, having been retained by independent companies to form a rival merger, a step which he finally advised his clients not to take on account of the impossibility of standing up against the Morgan transportation and raw material privileges.

From Record, Woodrow Wilson was fast gaining an understanding of the philosophy and technique of monopoly, as can be seen from his 1912 speeches, afterward published in book form under the title of *The New Freedom.*

As Gary and Morgan well knew, it was not beyond probability that, in case of Taft's renomination, the Democrats would elect a president who would press the indictment brought by Wickersham; and if opportunity arose, fill vacancies in the Supreme Court with men of the Brandeis or Stanley stamp, who would scout the doctrine of the good and bad trust and, like Supreme Court Justice Harlan, declare in effect that the only good monopoly was a dead one.

This, then, was the situation that confronted Morgan and his advisers as Taft's term of office neared its close and election day approached: a *volte-face* in the historic economic policy of the Republican party, which had hitherto favored big business in all its forms and deplored the Sherman law; a Republican party that had put its revised policy in practice by harrying the Steel Corporation despite Wickersham's promise (as alleged by Gary) to leave it alone; a Democratic party honeycombed with Bryans, Brandeises, Stanleys, and Wilsons, and predominantly agricultural, and which would certainly not extend the hand of friendship to the new and hugely lucrative Morgan promotions.

It was not strange, therefore, that Gary and Perkins, respectively heads of the Steel and Harvester companies, should have begun casting round for a way out of their dilemma, or that the plan that recommended itself was to sidetrack Taft and nominate a Republican, namely Roosevelt, who would bring the party back to sound views. Failing this, there remained the alternative of starting a third party which, though it probably could not win, would at least shelve Taft and rebuke his party for its backsliding.

As to the possibility of electing Roosevelt on a third party ticket, this was not so remote as one might at first have supposed. The activities of the insurgents in Congress, and the havoc wrought by the Payne-Aldrich tariff bill and the Pinchot-Ballinger controversy over the Alaska coal fields, had weakened the Republicans, precisely as similar factors—the oil scandals and the Hawley-Smoot bill—have weakened them more recently in the Coolidge and Hoover regimes.

In addition, the Democratic party lacked coherence and was credited with a talent for pre-election blundering on whose existence many people still insist, despite its adroit tactics in the 1932 campaign. Outside of the Solid South, warring elements—Tammany in the East and the insurgents in the West—hated each other as much as they did the Republicans. As it turned out, but for the accident of Bryan's desertion of Champ Clark in the Baltimore convention and his unexpected attack on Tammany, which forced the choice of Wilson (who showed himself not only a candidate with an invulnerable record but a matchless campaigner), Roosevelt and the Bull Moose ticket might have won by a neck in 1912, especially as Taft proved so weak as to capture but two states, Utah and Vermont, with but eight electoral votes between them.

The Progressive party, then, failed because it had an aspiration and no issue, that is to say, no described, understandable program for transforming its reveries into facts. In the second place, it failed because, under the leadership of Theodore Roosevelt, it attempted the impossible feat of reaching a goal through means that were politically antagonistic to the goal. It was always one of the Colonel's pet theories that he could perform this miracle—make men serve ends despite the fact that they disbelieved in them. To found a popular party with the money of Perkins and Munsey and promote it through their efforts did not seem to Roosevelt an impossibility, but it proved one nevertheless. It must not be concluded that Roosevelt

cared anything about the Steel Corporation or the steel men with
whom, since 19[01], he had had such close intimacy, nor should it
be supposed that the theories which Gary and Perkins imposed on
him meant a great deal to him. On the other hand, he realized with
crystal clearness, having lost the support of the Standard Oil interests in the 1904 campaign, that he must retain that of the other
dominant economic group, or as much of it as possible, if he were
ever to make another successful dash for the White House. Therefore, when Roosevelt was asked to free himself from the burden
which the presence of Steel Trust men and women in the Progressive
organization had saddled on him, a request was being made that he
was unable to comply with, even if he wanted to. Roosevelt was
shrewd enough to know that with the hostility of both the oil and
the steel interests, nothing but a miracle could land him in the
White House, and if he did not reach the White House, manifestly
his whole program of social and industrial justice, and the like,
would never be realized. He would use Steel Trust money and profit
by Steel Trust ability, but it would all be for a righteous end; and
then again it was to be remembered that the Steel Trust was a good
trust, not a bad one, and that therefore there was after all no antagonism, for him, between his ends and his means.

There is something strange about the power that money has over
us. If you take money from a man, it is not the baseness but the
very decency in you that rises up against your following any course
that will injure your benefactor. The average human soul revolts
against taking something and making no return.

The third and most interesting subject for reflection in the story
of the rise and fall of the Progressive party is the following. It is the
illustration it provides of the way in which the process of accumula-
tion of wealth by the politico-industrial means which I have already
discussed . . . seeks to protect itself. Here was an industro-financial
organization making a great deal of money through a process that
was forbidden both by law and by public opinion. Through its transportation differentials and ore supply advantages, it had reached a
pinnacle where it could prevent competition and fix prices. This, by
the way, is the much sought-after position that in the case of a pro-
ducer of a major necessity of life opens the door to an almost limit-

less acquisition of wealth. This important achievement, conceived and built up by Mr. Morgan, was menaced first by the appearance of Theodore Roosevelt, and second by the probability in 1911 that a new party would come into the field. Its high degree of vulnerability came from the fact that both the suppression of competition and the fixing of prices were illegal and that, galled by extortion, the public was apt at any moment to raise a hue and cry which might, conceivably, result in the dissolution of the trust, an undesirable proceeding since it would naturally be accompanied by investigations that would lay bare its methods, or in the possible separation from the Steel Corporation of the railroads and their transportation facilities, which were the main sources of its monopoly power. . . . The story of the rise and fall of the Progressive party is, from one point of view, a narrative of how the Steel Corporation went about averting a second danger and turning the situation to its own account. Even before the party's birth, men whose philosophy, interests, and works were inconsistent with a desire to create a bona fide liberal force in politics appeared unaccountably. At the birth of the party they were on the scene and practically purchased it before it had given its first cry of life. They paid for its keep, cared for its education, and went to the length of robbing its platform in order to keep it from error. They carried it through years of vicissitude and when, as the 1916 election approached, it was evident that the new party could not itself win, they used it as an instrument and finally sacrificed and destroyed it in an effort to force upon the Republican party Theodore Roosevelt, a man whom they educated to their own way of thinking, persuading him openly to champion the Gary price-fixing proposal. . . .

George Mowry

THEODORE ROOSEVELT AND THE PROGRESSIVE MOVEMENT

George Mowry is the dean of Theodore Roosevelt scholars. His important book, Theodore Roosevelt and the Progressive Movement, *was published in 1946, before the revival of interest in Theodore Roosevelt occasioned by the publication of* The Letters *in 1951–1954. Moreover, Mowry's work is the only history covering Roosevelt's post-presidential years which uses original sources. This excerpt from Mowry's book is an excellent analysis of the presidential campaign of 1912 in which Roosevelt broke from the Republican party and formed his own third party, the Progressive Party. In the three-way contest between Roosevelt, Woodrow Wilson, and William Howard Taft, the political programs of the New Nationalism and the New Freedom were openly debated. This election was a rarity in American politics, a real contest between rival political philosophies. Mowry shows that Roosevelt's aggressive campaign succeeded in influencing Wilson and in changing the course of American reform politics.*

The campaign that followed was a stormy one. Almost before the convention had got under way the first salvo of sharp criticism had been fired. Before it ended the floodgates of denunciation were wide open. The members of the new party were described as "liars," "thieves," and "besmirchers of honest men." Roosevelt was depicted as a "political anti-Christ" whose swollen and prurient ambition had led him beyond the moral law, and whose promises were as false as a dicer's oaths. The platform of the new party, according to the conservative press, was not an orderly program of reform but a long wild call to revolt. The Confession of Faith, screamed the *New York Sun,* "is a manifesto of revolution. It is a program of wild and dangerous changes. It proposes popular nullification of the Constitution. It proposes state socialism."

President Taft, at least, added little to the heat of the campaign. In accordance with his announcement early in July that under no conditions would he campaign actively, he confined his efforts to a moderate acceptance speech and two or three dignified public let-

From George Mowry, *Theodore Roosevelt and the Progressive Movement* (Madison: The University of Wisconsin Press; 1946), pp. 274–283. Copyright 1946 by the Regents of the University of Wisconsin.

ters. In these few efforts Taft reconciled his political position with his own true philosophical bent. For deep underneath he had always been a conservative. For a while in the first decade of the century, under the spell of the restless Roosevelt, he had thought of himself as a progressive and had even accepted the succession with the sincere intention of making advances on Roosevelt's liberal beginnings. But faced with the reality of office and with a widening fissure between conservative and progressive in his party, he had gradually found his true political level. Once there, he saw, perhaps to his surprise, clustered around him the Aldriches of the Republican party and not the Dollivers or the La Follettes.

Taft's campaign utterances of 1912 might well have come from the lips of Aldrich. In his acceptance speech on August 1 he deplored the reign of "sensational journalism" and the unrest of the people. He feared that social justice as then interpreted simply meant a "false division of property" which would approximate socialism. He denounced the recall of judges, the limitation of the power to grant injunctions, and trial by jury in contempt cases as vicious examples of class legislation designed to protect the lawless. His later written views approached toryism. For in defending the high protective tariff, in calling for measures to restore business confidence, and in his allusions to the law of supply and demand as it worked its inevitable way on the labor market, the president was simply repeating the fifty-year-old shibboleths of organized reaction.

In contrast to Taft, Roosevelt soon swung into a strenuous campaign of electioneering. Although he fully expected to lose the election and faced reluctantly the arduous labors of the campaign, he stuck at it with all his old vigor. A fortnight after his initial August campaign in New England he was in the Middle West. Two weeks later he was on the Pacific Coast, and by September 24 he was again in the Corn Belt. After a ten-day swing into the South he once again invaded the Northwest. While speaking in Milwaukee on October 14 he was shot by an insane man. From then until the last of October he rested, recovering from his wound.

As in the past Roosevelt's journeys through the country had been triumphal as a Roman warrior's. This was not the Roosevelt of 1900, for the years had left their mark. He was a bit slower in movement now, heavy around the waist; gray touched his temples. But he had lost none of his old power to attract the multitude. If anything, his manifest sincerity in 1912 and his ostensible abandonment of opportunism engendered even more devotion. At the opening of the campaign ten thousand people jammed the railroad station at Providence, Rhode Island, to welcome him. That night at Infantry Hall, with seats selling for a dollar apiece, thousands of people had to be turned away. When he visited Los Angeles the entire city turned out. Business closed down, traffic was completely stopped, and two hundred thousand people lined the streets to cheer him as he rode from the station.

Nor did the election lack the dramatic and the spectacular with which Roosevelt always managed to surround himself. The country grinned when it heard that "Teddy" had climbed over a tender into the engine of a transcontinental express to run the train for a space and jar the passengers off their seats. Even his enemies admired the mettle he displayed at Milwaukee when he insisted on continuing his speech after being dangerously wounded. Everyone applauded his magnanimity in protecting the would-be assassin from the fury of the bystanders. "Stand back. Don't hurt the man," he had shouted as the crowd rushed to avenge the deed. Even with a bullet in his breast he could savor the drama, and his mind shrewdly dictated the best histrionic tactics. He clutched a bloody handkerchief, held up for all to see. A month later Roosevelt wrote to Earl Grey with revealing candor: "I would not have objected to the man's being killed at the very instant, but I did not deem it wise or proper that he should be killed before my eyes if I was going to recover."

Throughout the campaign Roosevelt scarcely mentioned the President but centered most of his remarks on Woodrow Wilson. Setting aside his old weapons of irony and sharp sarcasm, he attacked his Democratic opponent with a gentle but devastating ridicule. Against the polished and literary phrases of his adversary, Roosevelt at least held his own. It was difficult for him to answer Wilson's charge that his election would mean the rule of United States Steel Corporation through the mediation of Perkins. Troublesome also was the prediction that the election of a Progressive President would cause legislative chaos, since the Congress would be Democratic or Republican. The renewed inquiry into corporate campaign contributions of 1904 may possibly have lost Roosevelt considerable support. Wilson scored heavily also when he attacked Roosevelt's faith in high protection. But in the polemics over two divergent philosophies of government Roosevelt was calling the tune of the times.

Espousing the tenets of Jeffersonian liberalism, Wilson had leveled one attack after another at the Rooseveltian concept of a master state almost without limit in its power to direct the economic life of the nation. He maintained that freedom of industrial activity was necessary for a healthy economic life. Roosevelt's program of regulation would inevitably lead to governmental sanctification of exploiting monopolies. What was needed was not the regulation of industrial combines but their dissolution under the Sherman Law and the restoration of a competitive basis. Such a bureaucratic state as Roosevelt envisaged would put an end to human liberty. "The history of liberty," remarked Wilson with his usual felicity, "is the history of the limitation of governmental power."

Roosevelt, designating such doctrines as "rural toryism" and their author as a sincere doctrinaire who delighted in professorial rhetoric, replied that such a description was true of governments up until the advent of democracy, but not thereafter. For what have the people to fear, he asked, from a strong government which is in turn controlled by the people? If Wilson's doctrine meant anything, it meant "that every law for the promotion of social and industrial justice which has been put upon the statute books ought to be repealed."

But Roosevelt's most effective answer to his critics was in his last speech before sixteen thousand people jammed into Madison Square Garden. Leaving a sickbed to deliver it, he made in this redefinition of his principles his greatest speech of the campaign and one of the finest of his whole political career. As he stood on the platform men noticed that this was a new Roosevelt. For once he immediately tried to stop the cheering, which lasted, despite his efforts, for forty-five minutes. He used none of the old sarcasm or the belligerent personal attacks, and the pronoun *we* took the place of the overworked *I*.

"We are for human rights and we intend to work for them," he said in answer to the charges that the New Nationalism would lead straight to autocracy. "Where they can be best obtained by the application of the doctrine of states' rights, then we are for states' rights. Where in order to obtain them, it is necessary to invoke the power of the Nation, then we shall invoke to its uttermost limits that mighty power. We are for liberty. But we are for the liberty of the oppressed, and not for the liberty of the oppressor to oppress the weak and to bind the burdens on the shoulders of the heavy laden. It is idle to ask us not to exercise the powers of government when only by that power of the government can we curb the greed that sits in the high places, when only by the exercise of the government can we exalt the lowly and give heart to the humble and downtrodden."

And then in the last moments of the campaign Roosevelt took occasion to fire one more explosive shot at his old enemy the courts. "We stand for the Constitution, but we will not consent to make of the Constitution a fetish for the protection of fossilized wrong," he exclaimed. "We recognize in neither court, nor Congress, nor President, any divine right to override the will of the people."

As election day neared it was obvious that the real race would be between Roosevelt and Wilson. Taft could expect little support from the reforming members of the Republican party. Moreover, the president had alienated a large block of conservative supporters. Many industrial leaders who had voted the Republican ticket for years agreed with James M. Swank, president of the American Iron and Steel Association, that the president's tariff and trusts views were heretical. For once a Republican administration was having a difficult time in collecting enough money to finance an election. When asked to contribute, H. C. Frick answered that he would give almost any amount to insure the success of the Republican party but that he did not care to contribute to this campaign because the administration "utterly failed to treat many of its warmest friends fairly."

As Taft's defeat became more patent with the days, so-called sober conservatism, fearing a Roosevelt victory, dipped its pen in hysterical and malicious abuse. Branding Roosevelt as the American Mahdi and his followers as wild dervishes, the *New York Sun* predicted that once Roosevelt gained the White House he would never depart. "As the Emperor Sigismund was above grammar, so is Theodore Rex above recall, except that of his promises and his principles." The *New York World* joined in the chorus by predicting that a second term would lead to a third, and a third straight to a tyrant. *Harper's Weekly* had long before warned the country that Roosevelt's election would be followed within ten years by a bloody revolution and the subsequent rule of a despot. But the depths of scurrility and foolishness were plumbed by George Harvey in an editorial entitled "Roosevelt or the Republic." "Roosevelt was the first President," it began, "whose chief personal characteristic was mendacity, the first to glory in duplicity, the first braggart, the first bully, the first betrayer of a friend who ever occupied the White House." From there it went on with equally bitter adjectives, referring to Roosevelt's "perpetual lying," his "shameless treatment of helpless women," and his willingness to grind the American people under the iron boot. "It is not the foreign war," the editorial concluded, "so commonly anticipated as a consequence of Roosevelt's accession to the dizzy height of unrestrained authority that makes for dread; it is the civil strife that would almost inevitably ensue from patriotic resistance to usurpation by a half mad genius at the head of the proletariat."

Those unreasoning charges might well have remained unwritten; for a Roosevelt victory was next to impossible. Since Wilson's nomination precluded any great migration of progressives from the Democratic party, Roosevelt had to depend upon the support of Republican progressives. They were not enough. Beyond that, traditional progressivism in the Republican party, unlike the make-up of the Democratic party, had always flourished in the agrarian sections of the country. There Roosevelt was handicapped by the fact that many of the progressive Republican leaders in the western sections of the country were either opposed to him or were content in giving him meager support from outside the ranks of the Progressive party.

Roosevelt's paternalistic philosophy of government was not agrarian but urban in its appeal. A high protective tariff, the regulation of industrial monopolies, the long list of labor reforms, offered little to the farmer. In fact the New Nationalism, in almost every instance, was the antithesis of the physiocratic, low-tariff, trust-busting doctrines of the farming West. It is little wonder then that in the eighteen largest cities of the country Roosevelt polled a considerably greater proportion of the total vote than he did throughout the agricultural regions. He was supported in the West not because of his New Nationalism but in spite of it.

Other factors stood in the way of a Roosevelt victory. Thanks to the party's "lily white" tag many Northern Negroes were alienated. The absence from the platform of an anti-trust plank antagonized not only farmers but many city dwellers who believed in the competitive system. Roosevelt's strict conservation views hurt his cause in the Far West, he was told after the election. Then perhaps most important of all was the lack of a smoothly running organization. Built up hurriedly in the space of four months it was woefully inadequate in efficiency and strength. No party has since the Federalists won its first contest in a national election, and the Progressive party was no exception to the rule.

In the November election Roosevelt at least achieved his desire to defeat Taft. By count Roosevelt received 4,126,020 votes to Taft's 3,483,922, obtained eighty-eight electoral votes to Taft's eight, and was second in twenty-three states while the President ran second in seventeen. Wilson, obtaining only forty-five per cent of the total vote, was handsomely elected. Armageddon had been fought, but the Lord had forgotten.

Roosevelt later wrote to Henry White that "it was a phenomenal thing to bring the new party into second place and to beat out the Republicans." Certainly Roosevelt's personal achievement, obtained without the support of either major party's organization, constituted an enduring testament to his own personal popularity. But a more searching analysis of the election figures fails to bear out his statement that he had brought his party into second place. Instead it appeared from the returns that there was little to the Progressive party save Roosevelt. Despite the fact that the Progressives ran a full national ticket in the majority of the states, they captured only one governorship and elected only a dozen or so congressmen. The results in the minor state and local contests were even more grave for the future of the party. Of the thousands of contests for local offices the Progressives succeeded in winning only about 250. These local results showed that with few exceptions the Progressives hopelessly trailed both their Republican and Democratic opponents. For example, in twenty-two states where Progressives ran for the governorship their combined vote totalled twenty-one per cent less than Roosevelt's total for the same states. In Massachusetts the combined vote for Progressive congressmen totalled thirty-seven per cent less than Roosevelt's figure. In other places the disparity was greater.

This condition of affairs presented an alarming problem indeed to the Progressive party. It is a maxim of politics that a national party lives through the medium of its local officeholders. Without the pecuniary rewards accruing from such petty offices, the courthouse politician, whose hand is necessary to maintain a permanent organization, soon finds other fields for his endeavors. No one realized this danger more than Roosevelt himself. And while he agreed with Garfield that the party had been permanently established, he was exceedingly fearful that the disintegrating force of four years without the sustenance of office would so debilitate the Progressive state organizations that by 1916 it would be a party in name only. "The danger in sight is exactly as you place it," he wrote to Robert Bass, "namely, that we may lose ground in the state elections during the next two or three years. We must do our best to strengthen our local organization."

The danger was not only that the Progressive party would disintegrate but that the whole progressive movement within the Republican party, built up slowly through a decade, would perish with it. Upon Roosevelt rested the full responsibility for the future of Republican progressivism, whether it would grow in its new environment to a dominant place in national life or would languish and finally expire. He had led a good many of the progressive leaders out of the Republican party just at a time when they had threatened to control it. Now sapped of its reforming element, the party of Lincoln was overwhelmingly conservative and was destined to remain so for years. After 1912 there could be no turning back. For by their desertion the Progressive chieftains had irretrievably lost their power within the party structure. If the former Republican progressivism was to be a vital national force after 1912, it must be through independent political action.

In November of 1912 the future of that permanent action was not at all clear. Judged by the elections there was no denying that the old progressivism had lost ground. Stubbs, Dixon, Bourne, Beveridge, all of them once powerful figures in the nation, had been beaten. In addition the results of the election in Iowa, Kansas, Nebraska, and New Hampshire, states where progressivism had once been the dominant political factor, left either the Democrats or the conservative Republican faction in control. Even Roosevelt admitted that the first result of the great departure had ended in disaster. "We must face the fact," he wrote, "that our cutting loose from the Republican party was followed by disaster to the Progressive cause in most of the states where it won two years ago."

Arthur S. Link
THE ELECTION OF 1912

Arthur S. Link is the distinguished biographer of Woodrow Wilson and the leading historian of the progressive era. His books include a history of the progressive era, a multi-volume biography of Wilson, and the collected edition of the Woodrow Wilson papers. This excerpt from Link's Woodrow Wilson and the Progressive Era *compares Roosevelt's New Nationalism and Wilson's New Freedom, the two political philosophies which dominated the 1912 election. Link also chronicles the election campaign: Roosevelt's opening attacks upon Wilson; Wilson's slow start; the genesis of the New Freedom; the gradual gathering of support for Wilson by wavering progressives; Wilson's defeat of Roosevelt and his assumption of the leadership of the progressive movement.*

Roosevelt's New Nationalism and what Wilson called the New Freedom mirrored a divergence in the progressive movement itself, a divergence far-reaching in its implications for the future development of governmental policies in the United States. As the campaign of 1912 became a full-dress debate over two conflicting progressive theories of government, it would be well to know what these theories were.

The New Nationalism was no mere campaign platform hastily contrived for the purpose of catching votes. It was, rather, the consummation of a steady progression in the political thought of Roosevelt and a significant minority of progressive thinkers. During the last few years of his presidency Roosevelt had set forth his develop-

From *Woodrow Wilson and the Progressive Era* by Arthur S. Link, pp. 18–22. Copyright 1954 by Harper and Row, Publishers, Inc. Reprinted by permission of Harper and Row.

ing concept of the federal government as a dynamic force in the social and economic affairs of men. His Annual Message of 1908, for example, was a clarion call to progressives to reexamine the assumptions upon which their program rested. This, of course, was in the best Republican, nationalistic tradition. Although Roosevelt by 1909 had adopted a program demanding broad federal economic and social regulation, he had not yet formulated a coherent political philosophy to justify such a program. This task fell to a then obscure New York journalist, Herbert Croly, who published in 1909 his *Promise of American Life.* It was easily the best political treatise to come out of the progressive ferment.

Croly's thesis not only summarized the most advanced progressive thought of the time but also became the rationale of the New Nationalism and even of Wilsonian progressivism after 1915. It might, therefore, be characterized as the philosophical underpinning of the modern progressive movement. In American thought, Croly said, there had been two divergent views of the role the federal government should play. The first was the Hamiltonian belief that government should intervene directly to alter existing economic relationships or to establish new ones. The second was the Jeffersonian view that government should pursue a policy of strict *laissez-faire* with regard to economic activity. The important historical fact about these two conflicting philosophies, Croly continued, was that the Hamiltonian concept of government had become identified in the popular mind with aristocracy and special privilege, while the Jeffersonian dogma of weak government had all along been identified with democracy and with a program of equal rights and opportunities. Croly admitted that the Hamiltonian philosophy had been used historically by the financial and industrial groups to justify special interest legislation, but he called boldly for an entirely new orientation in progressive thinking. What he demanded was nothing less than that the progressives abandon their Jeffersonian prejudices against strong government and adopt Hamiltonian means to achieve Jeffersonian, or democratic, ends.

It is impossible to measure the influence of *The Promise of American Life* on Roosevelt's developing progressivism. Roosevelt read the book with enthusiastic approval and it at least helped him systematize his own ideas. In any event, he at once began to translate

Croly's abstruse and heavy language into living political principles that the rank and file could comprehend. In a famous speech at Osawatomie, Kansas, on August 31, 1910, Roosevelt sounded the keynote of his two years' campaign. The old nationalism, he said, had been used "by the sinister . . . special interests." What he proposed was a new nationalism, a dynamic democracy, that would recognize the inevitability of concentration in industry and bring the great corporations under complete federal control, that would protect and encourage the laboring man, that, in brief, would do many of the things usually associated with the modern concept of the welfare state. "We are face to face with new conceptions of the relations of property to human welfare," he declared. ". . . Property [is] subject to the general right of the community to regulate its use to whatever degree the public welfare may require it."

This, in general, was also the program and theme Roosevelt set forth during the campaign of 1912. Needless to say, it attracted a large following, particularly among the social justice group and the social workers. As the campaign progressed, however, Roosevelt became increasingly radical and explicit. He began to place more emphasis upon the social justice objectives of his program—a minimum wage for women workers, a federal child labor law, a federal workmen's compensation act, federal intervention in labor disputes, an expanded federal health and conservation program, use of tariff protection to insure fair wages to workers in industry, and the like. In turn, he scoffed at Wilson as representing "rural Toryism," the mossback, worn-out Jeffersonian philosophy of *laissez-faire.*

In contrast to his chief opponent, Wilson had no such well-defined program or philosophy when the campaign began. He was at another important crossroads in his career, but it was foregone in which direction he would travel. For, along with his general commitment to the ideal of social justice, he was still a progressive of the Jeffersonian persuasion, undisturbed by Croly's challenge. Fundamentally a state rights Democrat, he believed the federal power should be used only to sweep away special privileges and artificial barriers to the development of individual energies, and to preserve and restore competition in business. The idea of the federal government's moving directly into the economic field, by giving special protection to workers or farmers, was as abhorrent to Wilson in 1912 as the idea of class legislation in the interest of manufacturers or shipowners.

At first it seemed Wilson would make his campaign mainly on the tariff, but it did not take him long to discover that this was a worn-out issue and would evoke no popular response. He seemed to be searching for an issue more appealing when he met Louis D. Brandeis for the first time on August 28 at Sea Girt, New Jersey. One of the leading progressive lawyers in the country, Brandeis was also probably the chief spokesman of the philosophy of regulated competition, unhampered enterprise, and economic freedom for the small businessman. And it was Brandeis who clarified Wilson's thought and led him to believe the most vital question confronting the American people was preservation of economic freedom in the United States.

Brandeis taught, and Wilson agreed and reiterated in his speeches, that the main task ahead was to provide the means by which business could be set free from the shackles of monopoly and special privilege. Roosevelt claimed that the great corporations were often the most efficient units of industrial organization, and that all that was necessary was to bring them under strict public control, by close regulation of their activities by a powerful trade commission. Wilson replied: "As to the monopolies, which Mr. Roosevelt proposes to legalize and to welcome, I know that they are so many cars of juggernaut, and I do not look forward with pleasure to the time when the juggernauts are licensed and driven by commissioners of the United States." Monopoly, he added, developed amid conditions of unregulated competition. "We can prevent these processes through remedial legislation, and so restrict the wrong use of competition that the right use of competition will destroy monopoly."

The divergence in Wilson's and Roosevelt's views on the role government should play in human affairs was more vividly revealed, however, by Wilson's savage attacks on Roosevelt's proposals for social welfare legislation. He objected to Roosevelt's labor program because it was paternalistic, because it would inevitably mean that workingmen would become wards of the federal government. Perhaps Roosevelt's "new and all-conquering combination between money and government" would be benevolent to the people, he

said; perhaps it would carry out "the noble program of social betterment" which so many credulously expected; but he did not believe
paternalism was the answer for free men.

And as the campaign progressed Wilson became more and more
convinced that the struggle between the New Freedom and the New
Nationalism was a struggle between two concepts of government so
radically different that he prophesied slavery and enchainment for
the people if Roosevelt were elected. "This is a second struggle for
emancipation," he declared in a supreme outburst at Denver on
October 7. ". . . If America is not to have free enterprise, then she
can have freedom of no sort whatever." It was Wilson's discovery
that he was battling for the old American way of life and his conviction that economic democracy was absolutely essential to political
democracy that gave ultimate meaning to his slogan "The New
Freedom."

One of the most interesting developments of the campaign was
the manner in which progressives reacted to Roosevelt's and Wilson's appeals. In the early weeks, before Wilson found himself and
his great vital issue, progressives wondered whether he was a progressive after all. In contrast to Roosevelt's warm appeals for social
justice, Wilson's early speeches seemed cold indeed. But as he
gathered momentum, as he began to talk in glowing, if general,
phrases of social righteousness and economic justice, many progressives claimed him as their new leader and hastened to his
support. The significant development of the campaign was Roosevelt's failure to unite progressive Republicans and progressive Democrats. The Roosevelt that progressives knew had many sides, and a
considerable portion of the progressives refused to believe he was
now sincere. "I wish I could believe he intended to do a single
honest thing," wrote Anna Howard Shaw, for example, "or that he
would carry out a single plank in the platform if he were elected. . . .
I cannot."

By the middle of October there was not much doubt about the
outcome of the contest. To be sure, Roosevelt had made a mag-
nificent campaign and had won the support of most of the Republican
progressives, especially in the Middle West. But he had failed to
draw progressive Democrats away from Wilson, and that fact alone
signified his inevitable defeat. More important for the future of

American politics was the fact that he had signally failed to establish the Progressive party on a firm and lasting basis. As the election statistics revealed, there was little more to the new party than Roosevelt himself.

V ROOSEVELT'S IDEAS AND IDEALS

Richard Hofstadter

THEODORE ROOSEVELT AND THE STATE

*Richard Hofstadter is a prolific historian whose works have generated much
controversy. His views on Roosevelt have undergone a radical change. His
first appraisal in* The American Political Tradition *(1947) amplified Henry F.
Pringle's psychological interpretation and ridiculed Roosevelt's reform pre-
tensions. In this selection from* The Age of Reform *(1954), Hofstadter sympathetically analyzes the progressive impulse in American politics; he shows
that while it is essentially conservative, it is also humane. Roosevelt and the
progressives feared revolution. They were willing to make concessions to
avert more radical solutions to the problems of industrial society. Hofstadter
shows that the purpose of Roosevelt's frequently criticized speeches was
his attempt to establish the government's impartiality. Roosevelt in his first
term successfully established himself as the President of all of the people
rather than the representative of any single class or interest group.*

The first major political leader to understand this need of the public
for faith in the complete neutrality of the powerful state was Theodore
Roosevelt, whose intuitive sense of the importance of this motive, as
well as his genuine personal sympathy with it, explains much of his
popularity. In this respect the most important year of his presidency
was 1902, when he brought the great anthracite strike to a successful
arbitration and launched the prosecution of the Northern Securities
Company. These moves, by suggesting that the country at last had a
President capable of taking a strong and independent stand in such
matters, gave people confidence. They were symbolic acts of the
highest importance. While previous Presidents had intervened in
labor disputes—Hayes, for instance, in the railroad strikes of 1877,
Cleveland in the Pullman strike—it had been as partisans of the
captains of industry, not as an independent force representing a
neutral view and the "public" interest. Now T. R. seemed in the
public eye to stand not only apart from but above the opposing sides.
During the course of the negotiations that led up to the final compromise, he loomed larger than either the mine workers or the
operators. At first he saw his independence as the source of a
considerable disadvantage: "Unfortunately the strength of my public

position before the country is also its weakness," he wrote to Lodge. "I am genuinely independent of the big monied men in all matters where I think the interests of the public are concerned, and probably I am the first President of recent times of whom this could be truthfully said. I think it right and desirable that this should be true of the President. But where I do not grant any favors to these big monied men which I do not think the country requires that they should have, it is out of the question for me to expect them to grant favors to me in return. . . . The sum of this is that I can make no private or special appeal to them, and I am at my wits' end how to proceed."

In fact T. R.'s wits were much more with him than he had imagined —and so were the sympathies of a few of the big moneyed men. Ironically, it was Mark Hanna and J. Pierpont Morgan, both of them paramount symbols of the public of the bloated plutocracy, whose help and influence made the ultimate settlement possible, for without them the obstinate mine operators might never have been prevailed upon to agree to arbitration. Nor did Hanna or Morgan expect in return any direct and immediate "favors" of the sort Roosevelt felt he could not grant. His own conduct in the affair, after all, was intended to fend off widespread suffering, mass discontent, possible mob violence, a potential sympathetic general strike, and perhaps even "socialistic action," and he appealed to these men primarily in their capacity as responsible conservatives who might be able to head off a social disaster. In the public mind the incident redounded much to Roosevelt's credit, and properly so. The historian, however, cannot refrain from adding that it ill accorded with the stereotypes of progressive thinking that "Dollar Mark" Hanna and J. P. Morgan should have attended as midwives at the birth of the neutral state.

The psychological impact of the Northern Securities prosecution was comparable to that of the strike settlement, though the economic content was relatively meaningless. This great railroad merger, which had been consummated only after a spectacular war for control between financial forces directed by E. H. Harriman and others directed by James J. Hill and Morgan, had brought about a frightful financial panic in which a great many personal fortunes were made and unmade. Of necessity the new combination had attracted a great deal of public attention, and it was everywhere known as a Morgan interest. To move for its dissolution, though hardly a blow at any vital concern either of Morgan or of the business community, was to appear to challenge the dragon in his den. (And indeed Morgan, offended because he had not been informed in advance, came bustling down to Washington to find out if T. R. intended "to attack my other interests.") The government's suit encouraged everyone to feel at last that the President of the United States was really bigger and more powerful than Morgan and the Morgan interests, that the country was governed from Washington and not from Wall Street. Roosevelt was immensely gratified when the dissolution was finally upheld by the Supreme Court in 1904, and he had every right to be —not because he had struck a blow at business consolidation, for the decree was ineffective and consolidation went on apace, but because for the first time in the history of the presidency he had done something to ease the public mind on this vital issue. It was, he said, "one of the great achievements" of his first administration, "for through it we emphasized in signal fashion, as in no other way could be emphasized, the fact that the most powerful men in this country were held to accountability before the law." Henceforth, whatever he might do or say, a large part of the public persisted in thinking of him as a "trust-buster."

Representing as they did the spirit and the desires of the middle class, the progressives stood for a dual program of economic remedies designed to minimize the dangers from the extreme left and right. On one side they feared the power of the plutocracy, on the other the poverty and restlessness of the masses. But if political leadership could be firmly restored to the responsible middle classes who were neither ultrareactionary nor, in T. R.'s phrase, "wild radicals," both of these problems could be met. The first line of action was to reform the business order, to restore or maintain competition —or, as the case might be, to limit and regulate monopoly—and expand credit in the interests of the consumer, the farmer, and the small businessman. The second was to minimize the most outrageous and indefensible exploitation of the working population, to cope with what was commonly called "the social question." The relations of capital and labor, the condition of the masses in the slums, the exploitation of the labor of women and children, the necessity of establishing certain minimal standards of social decency—these problems filled them with concern both because they felt a sincere interest in the welfare of the victims of industrialism and because they feared that to neglect them would invite social disintegration and ultimate catastrophe. They were filled with a passion for social justice, but they also hoped that social justice could be brought about, as it were, conspicuously. Men like Roosevelt were often furious at the plutocrats because their luxury, their arrogance, and the open, naked exercise of their power constituted a continual provocation to the people and always increased the likelihood that social resentments would find expression in radical or even "socialistic" programs.

Writing to Taft in 1906 about the tasks of American political leadership as he envisaged them for the next quarter century, Roosevelt declared: "I do not at all like the social conditions at present. The dull, purblind folly of the very rich men; their greed and arrogance, and the way in which they have unduly prospered by the help of the ablest lawyers, and too often through the weakness or shortsightedness of the judges or by their unfortunate possession of meticulous minds; these facts, and the corruption in business and politics, have tended to produce a very unhealthy condition of excitement and irritation in the popular mind, which shows itself in part in the enormous increase in the socialistic propaganda. Nothing effective, because nothing at once honest and intelligent, is being done to combat the great amount of evil which, mixed with a little good, a little truth, is contained in the outpourings of the *Cosmopolitan*, of *McClure's*, of *Collier's*, of Tom Lawson, of David Graham Phillips, of Upton Sinclair. Some of these are socialists; some of them merely lurid sensationalists; but they are all building up a revolutionary feeling which will most probably take the form of a political campaign. Then we may have to do, too late or almost too late, what had to be done in the silver campaign when in one summer we had to convince a great many good people that what they had been laboriously taught for several years previous was untrue."

Roosevelt represented, of course, the type of progressive leader whose real impulses were deeply conservative, and who might not perhaps have been a progressive at all if it were not for the necessity of fending off more radical threats to established ways of doing things. The characteristic progressive thinker carried on a tolerant and mutually profitable dialogue with the Socialists of the period, perhaps glancing over his shoulder with some anxiety from time to time, to be sure that Marxian or Fabian ideas were not gaining too much ground in the United States, but chiefly because in this age of broad social speculation he was interested to learn what he could from Socialist criticism. Fundamentally, however, the influence of such criticism was negative: if the Socialist said that the growing combinations of capital were natural products of social evolution and that the challenge they represented to democracy must be met by expropriating their owners, the typical progressive was only spurred all the more to find ways of limiting or regulating monopoly within a capitalist framework; when the Socialist said that the grievances of the people could be relieved only under Socialism, the typical progressive became the more determined to find ways of showing that these grievances were remediable under capitalism. In these ways the alleged "threat" of Socialism, much talked about in the progressive period, actually gave added impetus to middle-class programs.

At bottom, the central fear was fear of power, and the greater the strength of an organized interest, the greater the anxiety it aroused. Hence it was the trusts, the investment banking houses, the interlocking directorates, the swollen private fortunes, that were most criticized, and after them the well-knit, highly disciplined political machines. The labor unions, being far weaker than the big businesses and the machines, held an ambiguous place in progressive thinking. The progressive sympathized with the problems of labor, but was troubled about the lengths to which union power might go if labor-unionism became the sole counterpoise to the power of business. The danger of combinations of capital and labor that would squeeze the consuming public and the small businessman was never entirely out of sight. The rise in the price of coal after the anthracite strike aroused much public concern. And wherever labor was genuinely powerful in politics—as it was, for instance, in San Francisco, a closed-shop town where labor for a time dominated the local government—progressivism took on a somewhat anti-labor tinge. Where the labor movement was of no more than moderate

strength and where it clearly represented the middle-class aspirations of native workers and of business unionism, it was readily
accepted, if only as a minor third partner in the alliance between
agrarians and the urban middle class that constituted the progressive movement. Those progressives who lived in the midst of industrial squalor and strife seem to have felt that the best way of
meeting the "social question" was through means more benevolently
disinterested than those of direct labor action. Here again the ideal
of the neutral state came into play, for it was expected that the
state, dealing out evenhanded justice, would meet the gravest complaints. Industrial society was to be humanized through law, a task
that was largely undertaken in the state legislatures. In the years
following 1900 an impressive body of legislation was passed dealing
with workmen's compensation, the labor of women and children,
hours of work, minimum wages for women, and old-age pensions.
Even when much allowance is made for spottiness in administration
and enforcement, and for the toll that judicial decisions took of
them, the net effect of these laws in remedying the crassest abuses
of industrialism was very considerable. Today it is perhaps necessary
to make a strong effort of the imagination to recall the industrial
barbarism that was being tamed—to realize how much, for instance,
workmen's compensation meant at a time when every year some
16,000 or 17,000 trainmen (about one out of every ten or twelve
workers so classified) were injured. The insistence that the power of
law be brought to bear against such gratuitous suffering is among
our finest inheritances from the progressive movement.

Progressivism was effective, moreover, not only for the laws it
actually passed but for the pressure it put on business to match
public reform with private improvements. American business itself
had entered a new phase. Before the 1890's it had been too much
absorbed in the problems of plant construction, expanding markets,
and falling prices to pay much attention to either the efficiency or
the morale of its working force. American plant management had
been backward. But in the early twentieth century thoughtful American businessmen, pressed by the threat of union organization, con-
demned by muckrakers, and smarting under comparisons with the
most efficient managers in Europe, began to address themselves to
poor working conditions and employee morale and to the reformation

of their haphazard shop methods. Between 1900 and 1910, 240 volumes on business management were published. Frederick Winslow Taylor's interest in efficiency was popularized among businessmen. The emerging business schools, nonexistent in the country before 1898, provided numerous new agencies for discussion, education, and research in the field of management. Employers began to study personnel problems, consider devices for cutting fatigue and improving work conditions, and launched in some cases upon their own welfare and pension programs and profit-sharing schemes. Much of this was resisted by labor unions as an attempt to set up a system of paternalistic control, and much was indeed associated with the fostering of company unions. Few employers went as far as Edward A. Filene in encouraging labor participation in managerial decisions. But the whole progressive atmosphere did help to give rise to a system of private welfare capitalism alongside the statutory system of business regulation that was growing up. During and after the first World War this private system developed with notable rapidity.

So far as those important intangibles of political tone were concerned in which so many progressives were deeply interested, they won a significant victory, for they heightened the level of human sympathy in the American political and economic system. One of the primary tests of the mood of a society at any given time is whether its comfortable people tend to identify, psychologically, with the power and achievements of the very successful or with the needs and sufferings of the underprivileged. In a large and striking measure the progressive agitations turned the human sympathies of the people downward rather than upward in the social scale. The progressives, by creating a climate of opinion in which, over the long run, the comfortable public was disposed to be humane, did in the end succeed in fending off that battle of social extremes of which they were so afraid. Thanks in part to their efforts, the United States took its place alongside England and the Scandinavian countries among those nations in which the upper and middle classes accepted the fundamental legitimacy of labor aspiration and labor-unionism, and took a different path from those countries of the Continent where the violence of class antagonism and class struggle was heightened by the moral rejection of Labor. To realize the importance of the change in the United States itself, one need only think of the climate of opinion in which the Pullman strike and the Homestead strike were fought out and compare it with the atmosphere in which labor organization has taken place since the progressive era. There has of course been violence and bloodshed, but in the twentieth century a massive labor movement has been built with far less cost in these respects than it cost the American working class merely to man the machines of American industry in the period from 1865 to 1900.

Elting E. Morison

ROOSEVELT'S IDEALS

Elting E. Morison is the editor of the monumental eight-volume edition of The Letters of Theodore Roosevelt, *which brought about the reevaluation of Roosevelt's historical reputation in the 1950's. Throughout this volume the problem of Theodore Roosevelt's relationship to American reform has been examined and reexamined. Rather than becoming simplified, the paradox of Roosevelt is amplified. In many ways Roosevelt remains an historical enigma. Strange as it may seem, with all that has been written about Roosevelt, no one has yet written a full biography from primary sources. Morison, who went through every letter Roosevelt wrote—about 100,000—to choose the 10,000 that appear in the eight volumes—has as close a scholarly acquaintance with Roosevelt as is possible to imagine. His article, which appeared as the introduction to Volumes V and VI of* The Letters, *examines and speculates upon the ultimate historical questions concerning Theodore Roosevelt: What was his role in society? What is his place in the history of American reform?*

In one of his stories Sherwood Anderson sends young George Willard out, on the night after the annual fair, to sit in the grandstand at the Winesburg fairground. The sounds of the bright day and living people have been cut off. No hoof beats, no laughter, no notes of brass, no cheers, and no idle banter. A place that has itched and squirmed

Reprinted by permission of the publishers from *The Letters of Theodore Roosevelt,* Volume V, edited by Elting E. Morison (Cambridge, Mass.: Harvard University Press), pp. xxi–xxiv. Copyright 1952 by the President and Fellows of Harvard College.

and finally overflowed with the gaiety of life lies dark and empty. In such a time, thinks George Willard, there is something memorable, a sensation never to be forgotten; one loves life so intensely that tears come into the eyes, while one shudders at the thought of the meaninglessness of life.

There are occasions in history that provoke the same sensation. Certain countries at certain times have, like Winesburg fairground, fairly burst with radiant, irresponsible life. England in the Restoration, Bavaria during the more sober moments of the Wittelsbachs, and the France that was so skillfully lighted by those famous gas fixtures of the Second Empire; these were marked by a special sense of movement, a kind of noisy jubilance. Anyone enticed to a closer examination by this noise and motion may be disconcerted to find how little beside remains. Few useful insights, few moving attitudes, few fruitful concepts come down to us in the baggage train of history from these manic ages. It appears that when the noise died away, meaning died with it.

America has had such times—suitably modified in tone and hue to meet American conditions. The era of good feeling comes to mind and so do the nineteen-twenties. Quite possibly on judgment day, or even before, the first ten years of this century will be placed in the same category—a time of sound and movement signifying little. If this happens, it will be inevitable that the principal figure of the time will be cast into oblivion along with his period.

There are signs that this judgment is already in the making. Not long ago one critic announced that the stature of Theodore Roosevelt was diminishing year by year, and very recently an observer concluded that it would not be surprising if Roosevelt were sent to lie in the dark with Franklin Pierce and Millard Fillmore. This may be unnecessarily rude; but it certainly is suggestive. And there is supporting evidence for these views. It is true, for instance, that the Roosevelt administration brought to American politics a good many of the more stimulating features of the midway of a county fair. It is true also that interest in these features will not outlive the memories of those who actually observed or participated in the events of the first decade of this century. And it is also true that the Roosevelt administration did not contribute any of the massive formulations, either of intellect or spirit, that appear in the national heritage. We retain in our consciousness from these years no great releasing statement about the freedom and equality of all men; no strain of unearthly music, as from Gettysburg; no noble proposition to bring peace and safety to all nations and make the world itself at last free. A great many things happened from 1901 to 1909, but after forty years not much, at first glance, seems to be left. An attempt to discover some continuing meaning in what is left may appropriately begin with some comment on the character and personality of the principal figure in this period.

The surface manifestations of the President have long been obvious, and have been duly noted down—the energy, the doctrinaire morality, the curiosity, the zeal to organize and execute, the irresistible high spirits. What has been perhaps less obvious, and certainly less noticed, is that this spirited attack on life rested on no very cheerful or reassuring notions about the meaning of life itself.

There was, in many members of the generation to which Roosevelt belonged, a buoyant confidence in progress, a pervasive feeling that through the affairs of men there ran one great increasing purpose. This attitude Roosevelt did not share. For him there were only two reliable constants in human life—birth and death, the great antitheses that were embraced in what he called "the universal law of life." It was the part not so much of bravery as of simple common sense to accept these terminal points without morbidity and without illusion. For individuals and for nations there was a beginning and an end. What lay between was life—a series of unstable situations without plan or purpose superior to the intent of man himself. And this intent could be imposed only by human effort—by action, by struggle, and, if need be, by strife. For, as he wrote one of his sons, in a planless universe "the strife is well-nigh unceasing and breathing spots are few." In other words, life is a battleground for campaigns determined by man himself in which the fit survive and only those, as he said, who are prepared to die are fit to live.

Where this sense of existence as struggle within an unplanned and unstable universe came from is, in this place, incidental. That there was chaos in life he had, from personal experience, discovered early. His mother and young wife died on the same day when he was twenty-four years old and when he was forty-two he became President of the United States by act of a madman. No doubt also he found confirmation for his view in his patient and intimate observation of nature on western plains, southern bayous, and within the jungle. And anyone in his generation who took the trouble to read the Darwinian text unedited and unamended could find supporting evidence there.

It is not so much to the point to ascertain when or how Roosevelt came by this view of life as it may be to try to discover how, since he held it, he decided to deal with the experiences his own life presented. First he determined to accept the conditions presented by any particular occasion without, as he used to say, repining. "It is a dreadful thing," he wrote his closest friend in September 1901, "to come into the Presidency this way; but it would be a far worse thing to be morbid about it. Here is the task, and I have got to do it to the best of my ability; and that is all there is about it."

Sometimes of course there was a little more about it—memories and accumulated meanings that could not be set aside. Then one dismissed, not the fact which could not be disregarded, but the implications. Tell her, he wrote the mother of a niece whose fiancé had died, to "treat the past as past, the event as finished and out of her life. To dwell on it, . . . would be both weak and morbid . . . let her never speak one word of the matter, henceforth, to you or anyone else. Let her try not to think of it; this she cannot wholly avoid. But she can wholly avoid speaking of it." It was a counsel he himself had kept when he wrote the letter for a quarter of a century.

The second way to deal with this unstable universe was to struggle—that is, ordinarily, to work. "In the end," he wrote to Frederic Coudert in 1901, "the man who works dies as surely as the man who idles." This was simply the universal law of life, but the man who worked might leave something behind and he would certainly have found satisfaction in the doing. At the same time he told Coudert, "The older I grow the more I feel that . . . . the chief pleasure really worth having for any man is the doing well of some work that ought to be done; and I care less and less, as time goes on, what particular form this work may take." Over and over again—in public and in private—he stated his position. "Work, . . ." he assured the good people of Topeka in 1903, "is absolutely necessary; . . . no man can be said to live in the true sense of the word, if he does not work." And, as he was leaving office, he confided to his successor that his only religious feeling lay in the belief in salvation by works.

Some works, it will be recalled, there were that "ought to be done." How, in a world without one increasing purpose, did one decide what works they were? One had his own morality, if the world did not—an artificial framework that could impose a kind of personal order upon a scheme of things essentially disorderly. It may not have been quite as artificial as this suggests. "Right is right," Roosevelt once wrote Lodge, "and wrong is wrong, and it is a sign of weakness and not of generosity to confuse them." The moral structure was rigid; it gave little opportunity for the play of subtlety or sophistication; but it was a firm base from which to operate amid the uncertainties.

Taken all together, these attitudes, shorn as they are of any general philosophic interpretation of the meaning of life, present an operational approach to existence. A man after a careful assessment and a determined acceptance of what he takes to be the "real situation" sets out, without morbidity or unsubstantial vision, but with certain rules of conduct to make life work. At some length this private view of the universe has been considered because Roosevelt carried much of it over quite consciously into his conduct of public affairs. It always seemed obvious to him that "what is true of the individual is also true of the nation."

He began, in thinking about society, with an acceptance of its unstable nature. Like a political party, which he once informed an audience was like a sailing vessel, society was a bundle of incompatibles in which the separate elements were always struggling for supremacy and recognition. He then went on to compare the task of politics, that is social organization, with the task confronting the naval architect who must establish successful compromises between contending requirements—speed, strength, cargo capacity—to obtain the kind of ship desired. As with ship design so with social architecture, the problem was to reconcile "insofar as may be the opposing elements in society through the striking of successful compromises."

If the compromises were not obtained, the way was left open for the free play of uncontrolled energies. Throughout the letters published in these volumes there is discernible a brooding dread of revolutionary chaos. To Lyman Abbott, as to many others, Roosevelt once disclosed what he called his "horror of anarchy, disorder, and . . . wanton bloodshed." The way to prevent these destructive energies from coming into play was to find acceptable working agreements between the dissident elements that make up society.

How, as a practical matter, does one set about this task in politics? At the beginning it is necessary to recognize the real situation, to assess, insofar as possible without memories or prejudices morbidly brought down from the past or hopes too clearly prescribed for the future, the nature of the society one seeks to administer.

It is interesting to discover, in view of his background, training, and inclinations, how early Roosevelt decided that he lived in a world in which "big business had come to stay." Disliking and distrusting as he did the corporation executive and the financier, he was yet prepared to proclaim that America was an industrial society. It has been quoted before but it may be repeated that he asked his countrymen to look ahead and think about "the right kind of a civilization as that which we intend to develop from these wonderful new conditions of vast industrial growth." Of course he was not alone in this perception. But there were few in positions of authority at the end of the nineteenth century who recognized so clearly the extent to which mechanical power had transformed our life and customs. There were fewer still who were prepared to admit publicly or privately either the need for, or the possibility of, developing a civilization designed at once to exploit and to control the great thrusts of industrial energy.

Then there was the bundle of incompatibles contending for supremacy in this society. Down through the years from 1890 to 1918, at fairgrounds, in hotel ballrooms, over cornerstones, and from railroad sidings, Roosevelt defined the great antitheses in American life. There were the rich and the poor, the brains and the hands, the farmer and the machinist, the corporation and the private citizen, the company and the union.

How then to strike compromises between these opposing elements? For Roosevelt this was to be accomplished by the application of the Square Deal. The Square Deal was "justice, whether the man accused of guilt has behind him the wealthiest corporations, . . . or the most influential labor organizations." The Square Deal, in another effort at definition, was designed to secure "through governmental agencies an equal opportunity for each man to show the stuff that is in him," to give him "as nearly as may be a fair chance to do what his powers permit him to do; always providing he does not wrong his neighbor."

The significant words in the above paragraph may be "through governmental agencies." Roosevelt was clear about what he meant by this. "Good legislation," he once wrote, "does not secure good government, which can come only through a good administration." To Trevelyan in 1908 he was even more forthright. "I believe," he said, "in a strong executive; I believe in power. . . ." Justice between man and man, group and group, and the various incompatibles was to be achieved by the authority of a strong executive who apparently knew what justice was.

The limitations in this position—considered as a political philosophy—are disastrously apparent. It has no decent intellectual underpinning; in vain one scrutinizes the scheme to find a logically constructed system of ideas. There is no organized statement of self-evident truths about man and his requirements to provide a direction or a basis for judgment in political action. At anticipated worst this is an acceptance of things as they are; at improbable best this may be only a willingness to reduce inequities to a bearable point so that society may hold together while it edges along the lines of least resistance into the future.

Most damaging perhaps is that this operational approach depends ultimately upon no safer source of information than the intuition. The judgment about the nature of society, the description of the conflicts within it, and the selection of methods and times to resolve these conflicts—all these are the products of personal intuition. So also is the determination of what is justice. The Square Deal rests upon no more substantial ground than the intuitive feelings of the executive; a broker who thinks of justice as a satisfactory working agreement. No doubt the broker is honest and decent—he has said that good is good and bad is bad and it is weakness to confuse them—but he has set the bounds of honor and decency within the limits of what he himself intuitively feels is the possible. And he has, finally, determined that the acceptance of his interpretation of the possible must rest less upon persuasion or law than upon his own authority.

In the face of these limitations, it is necessary to proceed with some caution in attempting to find out what came of it all. From the crowded ledger of the Roosevelt years, three things may be extracted for further consideration. First, some surprisingly accurate intuitive judgments on matters both great and small. The lips that Lincoln Steffens said that Roosevelt thought with turned out to be quite sensitive instruments. As John Hay said, "he raises intelligence to the quick flash of intuition." Feeling, as he did, that the problems of the time were produced by the push of unorganized industrial energy, Roosevelt set about first to assist where he could in the passage of specific laws to conserve and develop our resources, to regulate common carriers, to dissolve monolithic corporate structures, in short to bring the industrial energy within an organized control. Anyone who takes the trouble to read the letters in these volumes will discover how carefully Roosevelt proceeded in his effort to obtain laws designed at once to satisfy the prejudices of Congress, to protect the rights of the public, and to fulfill the legitimate requirements of industry. And in these letters may also be discovered how he sought to strengthen old and to create, where necessary, new agencies through which the laws might be administered with speed and decision.

At the same time in external affairs, he discerned that the future of the country lay within the whole world and not in some insulated corner. He therefore, without nostalgic allegiance to a provincial past or self-deceiving and sentimental pretentions that this was the white man's burden, set about—insofar as he could—to equip the country for international maturity. The great island administrations of his Presidency were honest, sound, and without imperial illusion in seeking to encourage wherever possible the active participation of the island populations in government. In the Orient, in South America, in Europe he acted with decision and with flair to maintain the position or to express the interest of his country in world affairs. In further support of position and interest he sought by reason,

political maneuver, and indeed by guile to build a naval force sufficient to continue our policies by other means, should conference
and negotiation fail.

To some observers this shrill concern with the length of the battle
line suggested that Roosevelt sought to obtain his ends exclusively
by reeking tube and iron shard. There is no doubt that he respected,
perhaps unduly, military power, but he argued, in season and out,
that our real strength in foreign affairs derived from a combination
of physical, intellectual, and moral energy—that is from our total
national character.

No doubt in the field of international relations as elsewhere, the
claims were greater than the substance; no doubt, as at Portsmouth
or in the cruise of the Great White Fleet, the advertising exceeded
the product. No doubt, too, in 1909 the fact that this country had
begun to participate in world affairs was clearer than why it was
participating. Few indeed could precisely state just what point of
view we were to uphold in the family of nations. For Roosevelt, this
was unimportant. When, in foreign affairs as in domestic, the critical
situation arose—as in Cuba, Algeciras, and Korea—there would be
time enough to devise, within our scheme of moral and practical
considerations, a specific solution to fit the particular occasion.

The forty years since he left office have not really demonstrated
the unwisdom of these views. They have, on the other hand, disclosed a structural fault in the conceit that America can be an
isolatable quantity in the modern world. They have also revealed
very perceptible limitations in more doctrinaire, if more elaborate,
approaches to the conduct of our foreign affairs. These forty-odd
years have also uncovered no weakness in Roosevelt's idea that,
in the present state of civilization, foreign policy is sustained by a
force in being as well as by good intentions. "No friendliness with
other nations, no good will for them or by them, can take the place
of national self-reliance." As he warned his last Congress: "Fit to
hold our own against the strong nations of the earth, our voice for
peace will carry to the ends of the earth. Unprepared, and therefore
unfit, we must sit dumb and helpless to defend ourselves, protect
others, or preserve peace." He said this dreadful platitude a hundred
different times in a hundred different ways. He further did what he
could to obtain a self-reliant nation that would act upon it.

In reaching decisions about what he took to be wise and possible for the country both at home and abroad Roosevelt relied primarily upon his own intuitive judgments; but he took great pains to base these judgments upon information derived from other sources, notably from those equipped with special knowledge. He sought to obtain, on any given problem, the full spectrum of expert opinion before making up his mind. This is certainly in character. The executive who has no great faith in a body of principled theory as a guide to action must find assistance somewhere and where, more naturally, than in the minds of well-informed men.

A second thing to be extracted from the Roosevelt administration is the feeling for the single man—that man who was to be given as nearly as may be a fair chance to show the stuff that was in him. Roosevelt's instinct for the particular situation, his regard for the intuitive perception, his reliance upon the private scheme of morality all prepared him to look for the individual. He cut down through the dreary classifications of society—the farm vote or the white-collar class—to reach the single man; to snatch the individual from the ranks of cowboys, poets, hunters, mechanics, dukes, bird watchers, politicians, fishermen, publishers, emperors, engineers, wives, and small boys. With individuals from all these ranks and callings Roosevelt set up a direct two-way communication and relationship based on the stuff that was in both him and them. It was not good fellowship; he was in fact a poor good fellow. It was instinctive feeling that only the man himself counts. "While sometimes it is necessary," he wrote in 1900, "from both a legislative and social standpoint, to consider men as a class, yet in the long run our safety lies in recognizing the individual's worth or lack of worth as the chief basis of action, and in shaping our whole conduct, and especially our political conduct, accordingly." It is perhaps strange politics to propose that there are actually unworthy individuals—but it does help to recover for each individual a sense of responsibility for his own worth. How else to measure the stuff that is in you?

This feeling for the individual as opposed to the type springs from a view of nature that assumes that in the conduct of his own affairs man is the measure of all things. It proposes that he must be mindful of himself. This is a moving view of life that has profoundly influenced western culture. Today, in an age that thinks in larger increments—the little people, one third of a nation—this vivid awareness of the individual has a refreshing, and may have a therapeutic, meaning.

Third and last to be considered from these years is an attitude toward power. The problem posed for man by power and its relation to character and salvation has an ancient, unhappy history. Not Job, nor Machiavelli, not Caesar, nor Dostoevski has helped us much here save in description of the problem. Nor has experience. Only fifteen years ago a generation almost died with the words of Lord Acton on its lips. When every schoolboy knew that power corrupted, it was the fashion to suppose that the way to achieve virtue was to suspect all ends supported by powerful means.

It is idle to pretend that this question of authority is not one of man's great perplexities, just as it is idle to pretend that there is not real substance in the Actonian pronouncement. In the past, as it will happen in the future, corrupting influences have burst through the pales and forts of law and morality that have been thrown up around the seats of power. Yet stable social organization must still depend upon applications of authority. Theodore Roosevelt accepted this condition of affairs; he believed, he said, in power. Perhaps he believed too much in power, but he was not unaware of its undermining influences. He understood how some able men, like Thomas Collier Platt, were seduced by irresistible desires for control and he knew how other able men, like John Hay, disturbed by the implications of power, thwarted their own energies. In three ways, therefore, he sought to limit the corrupting influence of authority. He looked first to the law—the firmament of ancient custom and current opinion within which the administrator must work. But, though he spoke with respect of the law as a support for character, his respect was qualified. Laws were attempts at uniform solutions, while the specific conflicts in society—varying always in form and intensity—were sometimes better dealt with by executive action unhampered by the generalities of law. So he looked further for other safeguards. He found one in the limiting factor of personal morality, of character, the control of power by the control of self.

There is a tiny but suggestive episode that bears on this point. Two men were put in prison for passing Confederate money. One appealed and was released from prison by the Supreme Court on the grounds that Confederate money was not counterfeit. Attorney General Knox sent Roosevelt a formal order to release the other on the ground that he could not be held in prison for what had been adjudged to be no crime. Roosevelt, convinced that the man was morally a criminal, refused—"As for saying that I could not keep him in, why, he *was* in, and that was all there was about it." No doubt, he concluded, Knox had the best of the argument as regards the law but he had "the final say-so as to the facts and the man stayed in for nearly a year longer."

Roosevelt was amused; the incident was indeed amusing. But the executive had set the claims of his private system of morality against the law of the land and he had determined, at his own desire, the final say-so on what was fact. This is what Lord Acton, and many others with him, have been afraid of. In another episode—not so tiny —Roosevelt set up his private system of morality and his own desires against the usages of nations and the morality of other men when, as he said, he took the Canal Zone. There are arguments for him and against him in his behavior here—arguments that have already been put forward with sufficient indignation, humor, or understanding by others. The fact remains that he did indeed take the Canal Zone. For this he would never conceivably apologize, because he thought his action necessary. But he recognized the dangers of this attitude in himself and others. He therefore sought one final safeguard—to limit power by limiting its duration. When he told Trevelyan he was for a strong executive he also told him he was not for a perpetual executive. In 1904 he applied this theory specifically to the United States. "A wise custom," he wrote, ". . . limits the President to two terms," and four years later the time came for him to apply the theory specifically to himself.

In the spring of 1908 he felt, he said, more vigorous than he had ever felt before; he had thoroughly enjoyed the Presidency; there was no position for which he was better equipped or which he desired more; there was no one in the country who understood the position better or was better prepared to administer it than he. In the spring of 1908 he knew also that the Presidency was his for the asking. Believing all this, and knowing all this, he refused to ask; he even refused to permit the offer. To his sister he explained that he had always felt the Presidency should be a powerful office and the

President a powerful man and that the corollary of this was that the President should be held accountable before the people after four years and should leave office after eight years. To Trevelyan he explained more fully: "I don't think that any harm comes from the concentration of powers in one man's hands, provided the holder does not keep it for more than a certain, definite time, and then returns to the people from whom he sprang. . . . On the other hand, the history of the first and second French Republics, not to speak of the Spanish-American Republics, not to speak of the Commonwealth, in seventeenth-century England, has shown that the strong man, and even the strong man who is good, may very readily subvert free institutions if he and the people at large grow to accept his continued possession of vast power as being necessary to good government."

And so, against the conviction that he was better equipped than anyone else available, against the general clamor of the crowd and the organized pressure of the loyal and the ambitious, against the enchantment cast by power over the man who holds it, Roosevelt put the Presidency by for a season. Reckoned in purely personal terms, the decision of that spring was moving. It seems obvious from his letters that he was wholly tempted and half persuaded to continue while he remained fully convinced that he must make an end of it.

The point has recently been made by those who know about such things that Roosevelt's reckless energy, ambition, and insatiable urge to power were compensatory mechanisms for an initial frailty, defenses against profound neurotic doubt and insecurity within. The point is penetrating and instructive. It is possibly equally instructive to discover that in 1908 as on previous occasions Theodore Roosevelt could do what only the neurotic patient discharged as cured is supposed to be able to do, to control the operations of his defensive mechanism so that he in no way damages his environment. Secure in the realization that the law and private morality ordinarily put metes and bounds on his power, and content in the knowledge that he could in any case give up power, Roosevelt felt free to use it to achieve what he felt to be good purposes without paranoia and without guilt.

These distinguishing characteristics of the Roosevelt administration—the intuitive approach to situations, the selection of the individual as the primary object of concern in society, the unruffled attitude toward power—were not the exclusive property of Theodore Roosevelt. They were shared in and supported by the leading figures in his period—Root, Taft, Moody, and P. C. Knox in the Cabinet; Allison, Aldrich, Spooner, and O. H. Platt in the Senate. They were shared in and supported by, also, innumerable lesser figures in public and private life. If one tries to bring these characteristics within a single classification one is tempted, with some reservations and immeasurable trepidation, to say that they are part of the conservative temper, or at least that they are among the primary conservative virtues.

This definition was first brought to mind by a remark of Lionel Trilling in his admirable essay on the poetry of Rudyard Kipling. He points out that the liberal is interested in developing a body of principled theory in accordance with which presumably society may be ordered or may order itself. The conservative on the other hand, inheriting a solid administrative tradition, is concerned primarily with the governing of men. The liberal therefore tends to put greater reliance on the legislative process; the conservative on authority. This is all highly suggestive. Theory is concerned with general propositions; the governing of men is concerned with acts in detail. Theory is useful in producing general attitudes or understandings; it is not so useful in revealing the nature of a particular situation; such revelation is more probably the product of the intuition. Theory is useful in furnishing forth a continuing program for action; it is not so useful in putting the program into effect, which is the task of authority. Theory is useful in the development of a general concept about man in society; it tends however to remove the needs or characteristics of any particular man from consideration.

All this may indicate first that the conservative takes a far more particular view of life and politics than the liberal. He sets his insights, his own private moral system, and his own conviction that sound administration depends upon specific applications of authority from a single office or by a single man against the general theory and the general application of law that are the favorite instruments of the liberal. It also suggests that the conservative is interested in methods and the liberal in ends. The liberal with his principled theory is attracted by the opportunity to define certain aims or possibilities in life and to frame these definitions in law. The conservative shares Browning's view that life itself—the mere living—is enough. He therefore seeks, by compromise, by guesses as to what the traffic will bear, and by judicious applications of power, to maintain a viable situation. There are, no doubt, limitations in both views and no doubt both views are necessary in the development of satisfying social organization. And it is here that the conservative finds himself at a disadvantage. The liberal position is easily transportable, in a theory, a system of ideas, a body of law, into the future. The great liberal generalizations, placed as they can be and often are in statements of compelling beauty, may be handed down from generation to generation as influences and energies of continuing meaning. The conservative position is not so easily transportable. The concentration on method, the concern with process, the unorganized and virtually unorganizable product of intuition and insight in particular situations, the spare record of action taken, all these, rooted as they are in the contemporary situation, tend to lose their meaning with the passage of time. The most easily definable thing in the conservative heritage, the scheme of morals which the conservative uses in place of a body of principled theory, becomes, with time, a worn-out or even at times a comic anachronism.

In passing it is interesting to notice two things. The conservative, even more than most politicians, is at a distinct disadvantage out of office. Deprived of his main object, the government of men, and without what Mr. Trilling called a "body of principled theory," he tends to fall back on the argument that if he were put back in office he could run things better. This, as recent years have demonstrated, is something less than effective opposition. By the same token the liberal in office tends to lose his pure form. The exigencies of actual administration tend to force him to modify the chaste body of principled theory. It is a pity that historically the conservative has found it so difficult to acquire ideas, which are the stock in trade of the liberal, while the liberal has discovered it equally difficult to master the mechanics of administration. This failure of transfer between the two, no doubt as old as Mary and Martha, has produced no little pain and much more confusion in the affairs of men.

So one comes back to the beginning—to George Willard, rueful that he can retain no meaning from the cheerful day. Like all young men and many poets he asked too much; he was in search of some emotional response that he could recollect in tranquillity. There was none, now that the fair was over. And, in all likelihood, the emotion throbbing in the first decade of this century is now also lost in the night air of the past. But it is still possible, with some effort, to recollect action taken and to invest it, in tranquillity, with contemporary meaning. This presumably is one of the obligations of history.

In the administration of Theodore Roosevelt there may be discovered the conditions and nature of extraordinarily successful political action, not in a time when skies are falling or in the days of wrath, but in a time, to use a fine old word, of normalcy. This action deserves both recollection and analysis. The elementary investigation conducted here is something less than satisfactory. Some will demur at the selection of the evidence; others, no doubt, will disagree with the significances attached to certain actions. This is of no great moment. The intent has been only to suggest that in the administration of Theodore Roosevelt there lies open a fertile area of our past for an investigation of the conduct and the art of government. Such searches as may be made, involving as they do a concentration on process and negotiation in detail, will rarely reveal the highest aspirations of a nation, but they may well produce indispensable meanings for people determined to govern themselves.

Suggestions for Additional Reading

Most of Theodore Roosevelt's writings have been collected in *The Works of Theodore Roosevelt* (New York, 1923–1926). The Memorial Edition (24 volumes) appeared first but contains the same material as the popularly priced National Edition in 20 volumes. For the best bibliography of Roosevelt's writings—including most of the uncollected pieces—as well as for an exhaustive compilation of virtually all the secondary material see Edward Wagenknecht, *The Seven Worlds of Theodore Roosevelt* (New York, 1958). There are two critical analyses of the major as well as the minor secondary works: Dewey W. Grantham, Jr., "Theodore Roosevelt in American Historical Writing, 1945–1960," *Mid-America*, XLIII (January 1961), pp. 3–35, and Richard H. Collin, "The Image of Theodore Roosevelt in American History and Thought, 1885–1965," unpublished doctoral dissertation (New York University, 1966).

Theodore Roosevelt continues to elude the biographers, and no completely adequate biography exists. The most useful recent biography is William Henry Harbaugh, *The Life and Times of Theodore Roosevelt* (New York, 1963), a revision of the author's *Power and Responsibility* (New York, 1961). Henry Pringle's *Theodore Roosevelt: A Biography* (New York, 1931) is still useful, even if its debunking, psychological thesis is no longer valid. The slightly revised paper edition, however, regrettably omits the footnotes. Hermann Hagedorn, *The Roosevelt Family at Sagamore Hill* (New York, 1954) deals with Roosevelt's family life and Carleton Putnam, *Theodore Roosevelt: The Formative Years* (New York, 1958) deals exhaustively with Roosevelt's life through his twenty-eighth year. A recent historical and personal memoir by a cousin, Nicholas Roosevelt, *Theodore Roosevelt, The Man as I Knew Him* (New York, 1967) is interesting. See also G. Wallace Chessman, *Theodore Roosevelt and the Politics of Power* (Boston, 1969) and Willard Gatewood, *Theodore Roosevelt and the Art of Controversy* (Baton Rouge, 1970).

The most useful single item of Roosevelt historiography is Elting E. Morison and John M. Blum, eds., *The Letters of Theodore Roosevelt,* 8 vols. (Cambridge, 1951–1954). Included are 10,000 letters, several valuable prefaces and appendices and invaluable editorial notes and annotations. For the history of Roosevelt's time the following volumes in the New American Nation Series are excellent and include exhaustive bibliographies: George E. Mowry, *The Era of Theodore Roosevelt* (New York, 1958), and Arthur S. Link, *Woodrow Wilson and the Progressive Era* (New York, 1954). The scholarship on Roosevelt's foreign policy, not considered in this volume, is voluminous. The best starting point is Howard K. Beale, *Theodore Roosevelt and·the Rise of America to World Power* (Baltimore, 1956). For further readings in foreign policy consult the bibliographies cited above as well as the Mowry and Link volumes in the New American Nation Series.

For further material on progressivism and Roosevelt's relation to reform the following are useful: Daniel Aaron, *Men of Good Hope* (New York, 1951); John Chamberlain, *Farewell to Reform* (New York, 1931), Benjamin De Witt, *The Progressive Movement* (New York, 1915), Charles Forcey, *Crusaders for Liberalism* (New Brunswick, 1961); Arthur M. Johnson, "Anti-Trust Policy in Transition 1908: Ideal and Reality," *Mississippi Valley Historical Review*, XLVII (December, 1961), pp. 415–434, and "Theodore Roosevelt and the Bureau of Corporations," *ibid.*, XLV (March 1959), pp. 571–590; and David Noble, *The Paradox of Progressive Thought* (Minneapolis, 1958).

Samuel Haber, *Efficiency and Uplift: Scientific Management in the Progressive Era, 1890–1920*, is especially good on the scientific mentality of the progressives. James Weinstein, *The Corporate Ideal in the Liberal State, 1900–1918* (Boston, 1969) carries the arguments of Gabriel Kolko further. Robert Wiebe's work is essential to an understanding of the period, especially his "Anthracite Strike of 1902: A Record of Confusion," *Mississippi Valley Historical Review*, XLVIII (September 1961), pp. 229–251, "Business Disunity and the Progressive Movement," *ibid.*, XLIV (March 1958), pp. 664–685, and *Businessmen and Reform: A Study of the Progressive Movement* (Cambridge, 1962). Wiebe sees businessmen as sympathetic to some reforms and as leaders in much of the progressive impulse. The student should also consult Alfred Chandler, Jr.'s essay, "Origins of the Progressive Movement," in Morison, *Letters*, VIII, pp. 1462–1465, for a view of the middle-class small-town origins of the progressive movement, as well as Russel B. Nye, *Midwestern Progressive Politics* (East Lansing, 1959) for a view of the historical evolution of

American reform. Eric Goldman's *Rendezvous with Destiny* (New York, 1952) offers an overview of the entire history of American reform.

For the struggle with Taft see Archie Butt, *Taft and Roosevelt: The Intimate Letters of Archie Butt*, 2 vols. (Garden City, 1930). Butt was Roosevelt's military aide who stayed on at Taft's request in the same capacity; he compared the two leaders in frank, gossipy letters to his aunt Clara. Many historians tend to minimize Butt's credibility but the letters are worth consulting. The best treatment of the Taft presidency and its attendant political difficulties is Kenneth Hechler, *Insurgency: Personalities and Politics of the Taft Era* (New York, 1940).

For further discussion on conservation see Gifford Pinchot, *The Fight for Conservation* (New York, 1910), Elmo Richardson, *The Politics of Conservation* (Berkeley, 1961), Whitney Cross, "Ideas in Politics: Conservation Policies of the Two Roosevelts," *Journal of the History of Ideas*, XIV (June 1953), pp. 421–438, and J. Leonard Bates, "Fulfilling American Democracy, The Conservation Movement 1907–1921," *Mississippi Valley Historical Review*, XLIV (June 1957), pp. 29–57. Concerned only indirectly with conservation is Paul Cutright, *Theodore Roosevelt the Naturalist* (New York, 1956), a definitive study of a fascinating part of Roosevelt's life.

Two books that use the Progressive era as a takeoff point for perceptive discussions of particular aspects of American reform are Christopher Lasch, *The New Radicalism in America 1889–1963* (New York, 1965) and Otis L. Graham, Jr., *An Encore for Reform: The Old Progressives and the New Deal* (New York, 1967). Lasch sees a continuity of modern radicalism which is not simply confined to specific eras. Graham challenges the previously assumed continuity of American reform from the progressive era to that of the New Deal.

1 2 3 4 5 6 7 8 9 10